LIKE A VIRUS

A BOB RATHMELL

Writers Club Press

San Jose New York Lincoln Shanghai

Like a Virus

Published by Writers Club Press
an imprint of iUniverse.com, Inc.

For information address:
iUniverse.com, Inc.
620 North 48th Street
Suite 201
Lincoln, NE 68504-3467
www.iuniverse.com

ISBN: 0-595-09940-8

Printed in the United States of America

To Creg, lost at sea.

Acknowledgments

Thanks to Dennis for his support getting me on track to finish this book, and to my sister Karen and good friend Ron for their belief that what I was doing was worth while. Also thanks to Kate, Claudia, and Mike for holding respect for my work.

A BURIED BONE

*T*he man in the mirror looked strange and unfamiliar. Gary Nolan ran a finger slowly across the slick skin of his forehead carefully looking for clogged pores. Someone new was coming over for dinner, and he wanted no embarrassment from a blemish. For all his efforts, though, it seemed the more he tried to make himself look good, the worse instead was the result. The mirror was old, in parts, the metal backing of the glass worn so thin it gave no reflection at all. That might have been the problem, except the day before Gary would have said the mirror's defects added charm to his appearance, only now when he was nervous, did they seem to magnify that part of his character with low self esteem.

Frustrated, he turned away from his reflection and walked the few steps into the kitchen. From a simple cupboard designed and built during the first depression he found his special wine glass, stolen from a restaurant where he often ate because he had never seen one like it in a store, short, thick, perfect for a full-bodied red wine, a bottle of which he always kept on the shelf above the old gas stove. Placing the wine and glass on the counter, with a small knife he ritualistically cut the foil from the top of the bottle and carefully screwed in the corkscrew so as not to break the cork. Slowly he pulled, savoring the anticipation of a fragrant bouquet until with a "pop" the wine was finally allowed to breathe and he poured himself a glass.

A sip. It tasted good, and calmed him.

The sun was about to set, so Gary took the glass and his mood outside onto the small deck attached to the back of his house. Made of wood and built into the lacy branches of an old tree, Gary had built the deck to take advantage of the spectacular view of the canyon behind his house. For a long time his landlord complained the project would be too expensive until Gary offered to build it for free if the landlord would pay for the wood. It turned out to be a lot of work, but in the end well worth it since it was like adding a room to the small house, a room that soon became his favorite.

Sometimes sitting on the deck Gary would escape this world. A favorite fantasy was ancient Greece. The ambience was enhanced by the drooping leaves of the old pepper tree with its aromatic berries, but mostly by the two wooden pillars with classical lines his landlord had salvaged from a house being demolished and Gary incorporated into the design of the railing. After a few glasses of wine it was a spot worthy of the friends of Plato, and more than once Gary had conversed with himself there about the nature of things. That particular night his need to escape was strong.

Next to one of the pillars was a small Mexican clay fireplace on top of large terra cotta pot turned upside down. The fireplace looked like a wide mouth oven, inside of which the fire was built. A short chimney provided a draft to keep it going. From a pile of scrap wood, Gary grabbed a bundle of small sticks, and threw them inside. Carefully he arranged the wood so that it would burn properly, and when it was placed just right he struck a match and set it on fire. With still plenty of time before his date was to arrive, he sat back to watch the flames soothing slow dance of destruction.

Above him, the last rays of the sun vanished as the Earth's shadow moved slowly across the sky like a wand to reveal the glorious lights of the endless heavens through which we float. One by one the defining stars of the constellation Orion appeared. Gary was happy that despite the obtrusive wash of city light, which for most people made their lives the only thing in the universe, if the eye maintained a will to see, the stars still managed to shine. He sipped his wine, and looked up at them, and felt himself pulled into the greater perspective of outer space.

Near Rigel he had a dangerous and contemplative thought, one which collapsed the pettiness of his daily routine into the eternity of a moment. Gary's was not the usual way. He tasted immortality in his trances, but never appreciated their value by sustaining the flavor in life. For thousands of years the wisest of men and women looked to commune with nature in a way that would reveal a home and give peace to the soul in need of rest. For Gary it was natural. He effortlessly visited where few dared…oblivion it could be called, into God Itself. Security in things gave Gary no happiness. His joy was found spread thin across space and time. Content; he was amused that other people scrambled to attain what he could not help to achieve. A thoughtful soul, he knew that in this world that was not something easily understood.

Picking up a poker he returned his thoughts closer to the present and rearranged the fire. The flames licked each dry stick passionately, and with pops and crackles of excitement ferociously devoured the once living fuel. Gary sat entranced. Life from death, he thought, and so pointless while at the same time so pleasant to him. Strife seemingly absent, the fire burned properly as to its nature the wood into ash. It was done. The process finished. Except, Gary thought, by chance to be remembered in his mind alone, and then, not as something individual and unique, but only as a fire, as some abstract idea of what really was happening.

He put on more wood, and as it ignited he thought how quickly the age of self-interest was ending, and how a new age of history was about to begin. From every quarter he heard "freedom" as a word of importance, though at the same time those already "free" appeared to do nothing but conform to the crowd. Still asleep, the blessed dreamed contentedly of their great virtue unconcerned that while sleep was restful at any moment a nightmare could easily come to disturb their peace.

Gary wondered, how long can any people rule? Ideals grow stale with age, and in any case those in power usually distort their original meaning for selfish designs. Perhaps more to the point, most of memory is short-lived, and to him the time seemed ripe to pass the crown, this time to the nameless. Gary refilled his glass holding it up to the firelight to see its rich color. With a sip, he contemplated what he as someone named might have to give up in the new order.

The main issue for Gary was always happiness. For ten years he had struggled to construct a world around himself that would be enjoyable to live in. He wanted to possess little but few things of value, and then only what was "important." His job was adequate to pay the bills and gave him plenty of time to take care of himself. But he still wasn't always happy. People rushed all around him busily doing things that were supposed to be important or fun, so as not to be distracted by the sight of just how miserable they could appear.

Gary was a man cursed with vision, which he would gladly have traded away to find permanent pleasure in drink, sex, or even the movies as he envied his friend's ability to do. But nothing could blind him to the ugly truth of any lifestyle. When someone showed him their new fine car, Gary saw only the suffering of people in nations raped for the raw material to construct it. Or, when someone showed him a new dress, or suit, he saw standing before him the poor man or woman working late into the night sewing it together. No thing could give him pleasure that had suffering behind it. He didn't know about clairvoyance, but he could see.

Never reckoning himself self-righteous, he didn't care all that much that one man's good was another's misfortune. That, after all, was the way of the world. One should count their blessing while they can because someday they may be less fortunate. But Gary didn't recognize the blessing of his gift, the chance he had to use it to his advantage. He saw only the web beyond the good and evil of any situation.

Years earlier, when Gary was still coming into this "Consciousness," he had a moving experience. One day, driving home from work, he fancied himself turning into the embankment and ending his suffering once and for all. He had everything anyone could want. He was young, good-looking, with a job and education, and most of all a future. He could get married and have children. In time, he would be promoted, become successful, at least until he retired or was laid off later in life when the young ruled and saw him on the way out. And on the way out, he could not look back on such a life and be happy. But such a life bored him and so he felt that ending it all could only be a blessing. The desire to die scared him, perhaps because his will to live was strong, and so he left the life of his birthplace and moved out West.

The moving experience he remembered was not the drive west but came one day while he was standing on the beach under a crisp blue sky. He took a deep breath of the ocean air and felt like he just emerged from the sea the first self-conscious creation in existence. He felt individually important. And in that awareness vowed that he would never again indulge in self-pity.

With the Fates supportive, and a lot more honest hard work on his part, he forged that sensation of importance into a concrete reality around him. He trained his mind by going to school and watching the world, and he trained his body just as hard in the gym and at work. Gary was a good man. Slightly taller than average, his dark hair, hazel eyes, strong jaw, and muscular build that could be seen even through a loose fitting shirt, made him impressive to behold. For the training of his soul, he found circumstance to be the best guru. It was in himself that he found the support he needed to guide him as he grew as good looking in spirit as he was in the flesh.

During this period of his life all things seemed possible. The sun was brighter, and the sound and smell of things much more memorable. Each day was the beginning of a new adventure. And every night he lay down to sleep exhausted, not because he was over worked, but because he had lived life to the fullest. He felt immortal. God's creation was good.

Probably Gary would have never thought about the darker side of creation, at least not for many years, if it weren't for the friends his own age who began to die mysteriously in succession. The first to die shook him badly. And then too quickly, the next…and then the next one after that. It was war, but with no enemy. Yet to turn thirty, he began to realize that while life may be full of possibility, it is certainly the most fragile of things, and sure to end far sooner than any holder of it would hope. He began to wonder what was the point.

The fear of death, especially an agonizing death for himself, came to paralyze him. The only thing that kept him living was a daily routine that became his refuge. He ate the same breakfast at morning, worked the same job during the day, went to the gym religiously after work doing the same workout, and most important of all, when he felt uneasy drank a snifter of his favorite brandy just before crawling into a cozy bed at night to sleep. He bolted the doors to protect himself until one night while laying alone he realized how much like a coffin his room had already become. He let no one in, and no one could see more than an embalmed corpse lying before them.

He was a zombie, but grew frustrated with the wait to die before too long. At heart, he was a dreamer. He saw himself standing on a pinnacle surrounded by a pit of despair. Before him stretched a tightrope of hope toward the shining light of salvation. In his hands was a pole for balance, and so he began to walk along the razor edge most people were scared to venture; the edge of true experience, where dreams and reality mix to produce a heavenly life filled with love that knows nothing of pain and pleasure and can reconcile their opposition. With each step he still knew fear, after all, the abyss was deep, dark, and void of feeling. But the further he walked the further he left those he loved behind in the sanity of everyday life.

Ahead of the pack, he felt alone like a scout searching for passage across a desert. The light of the sun warmed his skin and gave him strength despite its parching effect. Around him, the view was sublime, though one not commonly beheld as such. His ears buzzed with the quiet, the silence of the place forcing his body to be still lest the sound of his own movement cause too much noise and pain. So he stood still, watching, his body resting in peace.

The quiet forced Gary to look inward and find in himself a being worth loving for the first time. And although it had been quite awhile since the now "mature" man bubbled like a child, he felt joy flow once again through his veins…though, sadly, the rush came only at times like this, all alone. Then, from the core of himself he had a realization—the task ahead was clearly to share his joy with another. Then the reality of his pleasure would exist beyond the fragile nature of his flesh. Through the shared experience of love which was outside of himself his soul would attain certain immortality.

To Gary's advantage, others saw him as attractive, even though most outside his close circle of friends, as a result of his striking good looks and charm, had rather to see him as aloof and unapproachable. His chiseled body and subtle mind were indeed something wonderful to behold and know, and yet, like any truly fine work of art set high upon a pedestal, one had better to step back and remain at a distance to appreciate the fullness of Beauty. Getting too close, or concentrating all of one's attention on any single part, was to sacrifice the ecstacy of becoming one with the whole— even though for most, to experience Gary wholly would seem much too much to take by nature.

For his part, Gary did his fair share to perpetuate the myth of his superiority. He had made himself into what all wish to become. And as long as no one looked to closely he knew others would believe he had succeeded. So he never stayed long with any one group of people, just long enough to barely be known before he quite suddenly became unavailable so as not to become old hat. His desirability was thus secured through this use of mystery. Though, this use was a double edged sword for it made it difficult for others to get a fix on him and figure out a place to fit into his life. And it made it hard for him to know what he wanted.

A good friend once advised him that his difficulties with others grew out of speech patterns he had which were not appropriate for casual conversation. If he would just learn to communicate with clearer intent, he was told, he might have more friends. Gary, however, was not convinced. Perhaps, he thought, he might become more acceptable at a cocktail party. But what he wanted was a different atmosphere around himself, unfortunately, an air that smelled bad to most in a land that believed only in the virtues of conformity and a heavy dose of perfume. To the ancient Greeks he might have been a god, but to modern day Californians, he was, to put it bluntly, a freak.

A loveable freak, and a character, to be sure. He was friendly enough, and a few people had even seen him infatuated and acting silly like a child, but then his mood could suddenly change, and without the slightest hint as to the reason why he would become sullen and serious: one minute an angel; the next, the devil incarnate. But always to his mind a man giving completely of himself, never once dropping anyone he ever cared for behind. The path of his life might change it was true, and if someone could not, or would not, travel with him they would just have to be content to see him off on his way alone.

No one who encountered him hated him exclusively for that conviction. Yet, the longer he refused to share his weaknesses, the more people in his community avoided what they perceived to be his scorn, and the lonelier he became as a result. No one realized how much pain their admiration from a distance caused in his heart even though they too were as convicted as he to continue on their way effortlessly living their ordinary lives, leaving the extra-ordinary Mr. Nolan to ponder what he had done so horribly wrong to be avoided by those he hoped to love.

On a typical Saturday night he found himself quite frustrated, torn as it where between his need to be true to himself and his need to be one with the crowd. Most of the time he easily avoided the problem by falling asleep early, exhausted, and with the consolation that the morning would bring peace to his discontent. The morning was his special time, a time when the ordinary still slumbered and the extra-ordinary, the free-spirits like himself, were free to stalk the world in their own way without expectation. In the morning he could be different as he wanted, and yet invisible to the prejudice of the average eye.

For to dissolve in this way was his unconscious goal.

A goal frustrated only by a form that yearned to be physical with the world despite his mind's conscious effort toward enlightenment and eventual release, to be touched in order to feel the tender stroke of another against his skin. Often, he would ache for such a companion. And the dread tension of worldly pleasure would rise up in him, hard and strong, and he would hate it and despise himself for such earthly weakness. At those times he wanted only to get up and travel and forget about the nonsense of becoming invisible and the foolishness of spirituality.

Yet, he was intrigued that dissolving in the crowd was just as effective a way to vanish, even if it was a kind of disappearing that seemed too easy and unworthy of a noble life's devotion. He hated that there was no greater difference between Nirvana and vulgar anonymity. But in reality their salvation was one and the same. And he could do nothing but live his life in the only way he knew how, and would live, regardless.

Whenever he did manage to "date" he felt that it must always end in disaster. To be entangled with another's purpose not identical to one's own for the sake of love, or just for the sake of sex was a sidetrack to be warily avoided. To remind himself of this he had taped on his bathroom mirror the warning: Venture from the Path at your own Risk. Still, he wondered why he could not meet someone to walk with him that was his equal.

Then, as fate would have it, he would sometimes find himself involved, and his life would become sidetracked exactly as expected, and he would long to return home to his own "weird" ways. The other would sense his frustration and eventually leave, usually after a scene, which would make Gary feel better for awhile…until he would again need companionship, and would sadly miss them while he felt sorry for himself.

He would miss them most as he lay alone in his bed on a cold night snuggled up under a warm comforter, a lamp over his shoulder shining a tight beam of light onto a work of long forgotten literature he would be reading to put himself at rest for sleep. He would miss them, until he stopped, putting the book down for a moment, to smell the fragrance of a candle that he burned on his night stand to clear the air and notice that everything in the room was in its proper place.

Gary was meticulous, with few possessions, believing the importance of a material thing was not its monetary value, especially in the eyes of others or as established by the law of supply and demand, but in its most careful placement and use. He looked around and saw his room orderly, and useful, and felt glad to be left alone in it.

Then, an altered view of his appearance would become apparent and he would burst and laugh out-loud at what seemed to be his "old lady" ways. Do "normal" men feel like this, he wondered? Or, do only my "kind" get off on something as trivial as order. Still, he loved the feel of his bed. And surely, no self-respecting "normal" man was in love with his bed, or loves the way his room is decorated. But then, he knew plenty of "odd" men that didn't as well. So maybe this love of place was just one more example of his peculiar nature, a nature that brought him a fair share of pain along with it's pleasure.

Contradiction was Gary's middle name. He often fluctuated between two extremes of motivation and behavior. One part of himself very much wanting to realize an ideal about living a good life, while another part wanted only to experience life to the fullest without having to always think about it. Even his thinking side was well aware that in the end he would eventually have to give up all analysis and just live his "good" life without reason. But Gary could not so easily give up the effort of the search for truth. He was never sure he knew enough to relax and succeed.

As part of his conscious effort to move his body more into the world and merge with others, Gary, tried to date people on a regular basis. In March of that year, the weather in Southern California had been unseasonable warm and he went often to the beach, a great place to meet people. The air was clear, the sun warm, and you could get a good view of what you were getting into so to speak. It was easier there to strike up a conversation. If Gary went out to a bar and tried to do the same thing he had to get shit-faced drunk in order to get up the nerve to talk to someone he didn't know. But at the beach, something about the dreamlike effect of the crashing surf was all that was needed to be friendly.

One afternoon Gary, by chance, since he didn't know beforehand who would be at the beach, and later by some foresight and careful placement of his towel, in order to catch the eye of someone who caught his interest, he met Kim. Circumstance didn't allow for them to get together again or have sex then in March, but they had at least got to know each other, and Gary later found out that Kim was an acquaintance of another friend of his named John.

One of John's favorite things to do was to go to an "alternative" dance club on Friday nights. And he always asked Gary to join him, even though most of the time Gary had some lame excuse not to go. Really, he was more anxious about going, and would grow sleepy early in the evening in order to give himself the perfect, if all too "tired" excuse of exhaustion.

One Friday night toward the end of October, however, Gary had to work late and found his convenient excuse of no use. And since he really wanted to go out anyway, especially since John had mentioned that he often saw Kim at the bar, Gary, quite bravely spurred on by hormones, took the big step toward adventure.

The bar was within walking distance from his house, and the night sky that evening was unusually spectacular for a stroll. Wisps of low clouds illuminated by the lights of the city moved below and around the starry lights of heaven beyond. There was so much going on up there and Gary was just the kind of oddball to take notice of it. He breathed in deeply of the crisp fall air, and felt proud of himself for finally doing something positive in his life. It wasn't in the end all that difficult, and while his expectations were rather modest, he did look forward to having a good time.

Inside the club the music was loud and the conversation level so noisy it made hearing someone talk impossible. Gary, at first a little self-conscious, stood in line at the bar to buy a beer. His eyes tried to scan the room to see if he knew anyone without looking too obvious. While, of course, at the same time many other eyes were checking him out, someone new not wearing black venturing sheepishly into a progressive rock-and-roll bar.

"I'm out of place," he thought. Then, the self-confidence building response, "No. I live near by. My friend invited me here. I have every right to be here."

He finally got his beer and took a quick gulp off the top. Moving away from the bar to find a securer place to stand, John quickly came strolling over, his salvation.

"Hey, Gary, good to finally see you out," he said in warm greeting.

"Yep," grunted Gary. "Finally made it."

"Good! You know, Kim's here. And asking about you again."

"Really?" said Gary, coolly looking around the room for a glimpse of his potential love. It had been some time since they met at the beach and his mental image of his affection had grown somewhat dim, especially since the sun can cast a much different light on a person than the dim light of a bar.

John motioned toward the dance floor, and there amidst the swirling lights of a pretentious dance heaven, moved the gorgeous Kim with a blond boy that was cute. Gary almost felt jealous. After all, he was not so young, soon to turn thirty, and his hair was black and somewhat receding. His facial features were no longer smooth but roughed with experience, which most times he liked well enough, but at times like this made him feel less than perfect.

"Are those two dating?" he asked John.

"I don't think so," said his friend sensing Gary's discomfort. "They're always here together. But I don't know their story for sure."

But then, as if he knew he was being talked about, Kim glanced over in Gary and John's direction and a big smile crossed his face. He motioned his buddy to stop and the two of them moved off the dance floor dripping with sweat.

"Finally," said Kim out of breath to Gary with a warm smile.

"So we meet again," Gary responded awkwardly. "John tells me you're here often."

Small talk was not Gary's specialty, but it didn't matter. It was clear that Kim was glad to see him. And after Kim introduced his friend Charley to John and Gary, John and Charley went to the bar to get a drink leaving the two new friends conveniently "alone" to get better acquainted. Gary couldn't help noticing a slight twinge of what seemed jealousy in Charley's stare.

Later, he would learn harshly that he was flattering himself with such simple-minded self-centered analysis. Charley was a bar buddy of Kim, their relationship quite stable and well defined. What Gary had seen in Charley's disinterest was not the loathing of a rival, but the bored look of someone who had seen the same thing happen all too many times before.

Kim smiled at Gary and patted him on his firm butt. "Nice ass," he said smacking his lips.

Normally, such a rude compliment would have offended Gary, even though he was well aware he had a "nice ass." For that to be the first thing for someone he liked to notice seemed a bit degrading to his ego. Of course, in fairness to Kim, Gary had worn the tightest pair of jeans he owned that evening.

The rest of the night didn't amount to much. Gary got Kim's number, and they both said they wanted to get together. Gary even thought about inviting his new friend home after the bar closed, but long before he ever got a chance to bring up the subject, Charley decided he wanted to go somewhere else to party. No problem, thought Gary, Charley was nice enough, but more in the way than not. If he went somewhere else, that would be just fine with him.

But it didn't turn out to be so great because Kim had come to the bar in Charley's car. His car, he said, had oil spilled all over the passenger seat so someone else always had to drive him around. Gary could have said that he would give Kim a ride home, but that would make his casual invitation seem somewhat more desperate, being it was after all the first night they had met officially.

Gary talked to John about the lousy music the D.J. was playing. And when Kim finally came over to him to apologize for leaving so soon after they had just met, Gary said, he thought appropriately, that it was good to have even seen him at all. After all, Kim had no way of knowing that he would see Gary out that night, and if Gary were Charley, he certainly wouldn't like it if his friend hitched up with some trick and ditched him out alone so casually.

Though despite his detached words, walking home alone made him feel differently. He was frustrated, wanting something, but not knowing what exactly would make him happy. He thought maybe he was just drunk, and that he would, as usual, feel better the next day. He was right, of course, not about being drunk, because he wasn't that drunk after only two beers, but that he would feel better in the morning. He would feel better because in the morning he would have buried the previous night deep in his unconscious, to blindly start living a new day as if from scratch.

The next day Gary called Kim late in the afternoon and asked him if he would come over for dinner. And Kim sounded genuinely happy to hear Gary call. They set the time for around 7:30, and Gary said he would make dinner at his house, so that they would have a chance to talk.

Now, he sat before the fire. Kim was very late.

At first, Gary wanted to get upset. He thought, surely he must come soon, or at least call, though a premonition warned him that perhaps Kim was not going to show up at all. What was it about the conversation on the phone that made him feel this way? Was it that Kim had taken so much pride in the fact that he never arrived anywhere on time? To be late was rude in Gary's mind. It was a display of self-centered arrogance that put down those that were left waiting. Normally, if it hadn't been so long since a real date for Gary, he would have never put up with such arrogance. But Kim was cute, and that was probably why he thought he could just about get away with anything.

The fire roared.

Looking at the flames flicker placed Gary in a restful state of mind. The rush from the wine helped to alter his consciousness. For a moment, he even forgot about Kim being late for dinner. His skill at rest returned, and with it a quality of peace. When he would be still in the moment, Gary had an uncanny gift to draw into his mind knowledge about himself. Nothing mystical about it, in stillness, Gary was simply able to see his life out of context, which was a skill most useful in accurate self-reflection.

High above the horizon the brilliant light of the planet Saturn shone as the beacon of the night sky and direction for his meditation. Its light pulled his attention up into the heavens where the planets and stars where a constant fascination. It was his pet project to sense where he stood in the physical universe from their perspective.

What he wanted was no less than to understand his life from the perspective of God, not satisfied with the puny knowledge of a person dizzied by the spin of Earth as it voyaged through space. Human culture was no help. City lights had long ago moved the dome of heaven in close around humanity, erasing the problem, instead of clarifying it. From the city, it was hard to look up into the sky and think about where everything would be, if he were somewhere else in space and time watching it all from a distance.

But the will of Saturn was stronger than this human bent toward denial. Always steady, it moved so slowly across the background of stars that it took nearly thirty years to return to the same place in the sky. Of course, from Earth it appeared to move erratically, sometimes, not at all, especially to those whose interest was little. But to see the planet move steadily, as Gary had done patiently for the past few years, was a humbling experience.

Far out in space it traveled, oblivious to the melodrama of Earthly life, yet somehow still very much involved through the weak but amazing force of gravity. It's huge weight was a constant pull on Gary like, he speculated, the unconditional love of God. The love of Saturn was constant, and no matter what his mood, Gary could look up into the sky and see It shining there in order, ignoring him it was true, but loving him all the same when he took the time to come home and feel it.

As the fire warmed him, this power of love from the natural order reduced him to joyful tears.

"I am complete," he whispered. "I could now die happy."

Then his spirit flew off to Saturn and sat proudly on the edge of its rings. The tiny, bluish star of the Earth shown far off in the distance. He felt content not to be involved with the melodrama of her history. Nothing happening there was all that important out here in space; and it was wonderful, not frightening to admit it. He was nothing it was true, and yet, he was more than everything in order to have that realization.

A blink of the eye, and he found himself back on his deck. Above him, the rare sight in town of a fireball shot across the night sky, its exciting light catching his eye which stayed fixed on the afterglow of its tail. Simultaneously, a pop from the fire sent a small hot amber flying onto the cold skin of his hand. It burned a little, but he kept looking skyward. The two events were connected, as if by magic a bone from heaven had been thrown down, a bone by instinct Gary dutifully buried into the backyard of his soul. He did this unconsciously, and as a result, would have trouble finding the right spot to dig it back up. Lifting his glass he took one last sip of wine, and wondered why he had to wipe off the tears from his face.

Getting up, Gary walked back into the house, the hour now made it clear that he had been stood up for certain. He sadly finished preparing dinner for himself.

"Kim's loss," he thought. Then, "My loss too…I can be friends with God, but no man."

Just then the phone rang. His heart pounded. Ready to forgive him, he anxiously hoped it would be Kim.

"Hello," he choked.

"Gary?…" It was the voice of a woman. "This is Charlene. Are you busy?"

"Me busy?" he said sarcastically with a chuckle. "It's just Saturday night, why should I be busy?"

"Well, you're such a hot stud."

"Oh, that's right. Is that why you called, to remind me?"

"No. What I called for was to ask if you'd like to go to San Felipe with Josh and me next weekend? Anton's going to let us all stay at his place, and I think you'd like it there."

"You know," said Gary, "it's my birthday next weekend."

"Yes, I know. Did you have other plans?"

"No."

"Then you'll come?"

"It sounds fun."

"Great! I'll call you sometime next week about the details." She paused, "Are you sure you're all right? You sound kinda sad."

"Yeah, I'm Okay," he lied, not wanting to share all his feelings at that time with his good friend. "And thanks for calling. I'll talk to you soon."

As he put down the phone Gary could not help smiling. All things considered, he was quite a lucky man, in spite of all the time he wasted feeling sorry for himself.

SAN FELIPE

Joshua drove to his girlfriend's for the night. On the way, he took a familiar detour through the park. The moon, low on the horizon, cast long sinewy shadows of light and dark through the trees, light, with the ethereal effect of a dream, dark, with the mystery of that which is unknown. The headlights of his car reflected their harsher, more civilized light off the dividing line of the road, focusing his attention in close, making what was beyond, and what was off to the side, look even darker than without their advantage. This mattered little to Josh, who knew the way instinctively. Ahead, he saw the public restroom, well lit, and pulled his car off to the side and parked. The engine quiet, he sat still for a moment allowing his eyes to adjust to the night.

In the rear-view mirror he glimpsed a shadow gliding slowly across the lawn toward him. The dark form reached up and softly tapped the window. Josh could see a man gesture for a cigarette. Fearful to have someone so close looking in on him, he shook his head no, and then turned to adjust his radio pretending to ignore the beggar. The man, use to rejection, walked off into the shadow of a tree, and stood there seeming to become part of its trunk. He finally disappeared, and even though Josh knew he was still there, as were many others, not seeing them made him feel anonymous again.

This part of the park was a place to find quick, casual, sex with another man on demand. Josh, though, did not consider himself a homosexual; just horny at times. Like a hunter he watched the shadows move mysteriously through the trees and wondered what they were about, if he could conquer, take what he wanted from them, then move on without any strings of attachment. At the proper time he got out of his car he began to walk up the hill, stepping carefully so as not to make a sound. Sometimes, Josh got the greatest pleasure just watching other people doing it.

But his first pass through the grove of trees was unfruitful. It was hard to tell what to expect in the park at night. Most times it would be extremely dull, but once in a while it could be so exciting that the pleasure from that one good time would keep him coming until it happened again. He decided to move out into the clear and sit on a grassy hill that overlooked but was not a part of the mainstream of activity. The temperature was pleasant and it felt good to be out-of-doors. Sometimes, he wondered if that wasn't the real reason he enjoyed himself there.

Suddenly, from down by his car, he was disturbed to hear a shriek of terror. The loudness of the cry ripped open the peace of the place and made him freeze and take note of the situation. Frozen, except for the uncontrollable shivering his body began to manifest, he felt safe enough in the shadows. And, such excitement was after all part of the reason why he ventured there in the first place.

"AAARRREEEE!!!" yelled the monster.

Josh could see the source of the commotion down near his car. The man shouting was standing on top of a picnic table swinging his arms under the one street lamp in the area.

Josh decided to move behind a thick Eucalyptus tree to conceal himself and get a better view of the action.

Near the yelling man two shadows moved apart and away from him.

"God hates fags!" the demon yelled in their direction.

Josh hated the word faggot. It disturbed him to hear it used especially in a condescending way. Not that his personal manliness was threatened. He had a girlfriend to make sure of that. But sometimes he yearned for something less intense, and the guys in the park were good for that and friendly, so he would come at night, for a little fun.

And that's all it was—fun. He never thought anymore about it. It was quick, finished, and forgotten by the time he cleaned himself off. Then he could sleep like a baby, knowing that his secret life was just that. His girl wouldn't care much, anyway. She loved him a lot, and he loved her too. He came to the park often, but if anyone would have known to ask him about it, he would have easily denied it, living securely inside the walls of his own lie.

Then, a police car moved slowly down the service road casting a different light into the darkness. It stopped near the culprit which Josh found amusing because normally it was the police who caused the harassment of people trying to make out. But that night they came as the friends of the shadows. Even so, Josh felt uneasy with their presence and stole back to his car, to get on to the security and normality of his bed and some sleep.

The next day he planned to drive down into Mexico for a weekend holiday.

Gary arrived at Charlene's house early, as usual. She, equally as predictable, was late getting ready. And Josh, her boyfriend and lover, was right behind her in style.

"Get yourself a cup of coffee," said Charlene in welcome as she pulled her hair back and moved to her bedroom to finish putting on her makeup. "I'm just about ready."

Gary had already had a cup of coffee but took another against his better judgment and followed her apologizing, "Sorry if I came too early."

"No, no. You're not too early. I wanted to talk to you anyway." She motioned for Gary to come sit near her. They looked at each other through her vanity mirror. "Since Josh and I got together we haven't had much time for each other."

"I know," said Gary sadly. "I do miss the good times we used to have."

Charlene suspected Gary's dejection extended beyond their changing friendship. "What's the matter?" she asked, as she moved ritualistically to outline an eye.

"Nothing," said Gary.

She waited patiently for more, before outlining the other.

Her pause of tolerance forced him to keep speaking. "Well," he said, "I am feeling a little out of place, that's all. Nothing I do seems right for me to have any friends."

Charlene giggled. "I don't know, considering some of the friends I have, you might be doing better than you realize."

"It's not that I want just any friends. There must be some people out there who are like me, that I can relate to."

"Well," she turned from the mirror and looked him straight in the eye, "I'm here, aren't I."

"Yeah," he blushed ashamed, "I know. But that's not exactly what I mean."

"Hun, what do you mean? It's easy to wish for something you don't have to solve all your problems. But do you really know what it is you're looking for?"

He aimlessly fiddled with a bottle of nail polish, then conceded, "Probably not."

"Well," she consoled, "I doubt if we can solve this problem in a few minutes, and let's not worry about it this weekend. It's your birthday, and this is supposed to be a vacation. I think you're going to like Anton's place. Everything's so different down in Mexico."

Anton and Josh arrived by the time Gary walked back outside to get his bags out of his car and Charlene finished making herself up. Gary watched enviously as Josh gave Charlene a big kiss. "Easy for her to talk," he thought without even a hint of malice. Her words were surely universal, but her circumstance did make them easier to say. Josh was a good look-ing man, and from what little Gary knew, a good man also, which in his mind was the real prize. He knew all too well how shallow beauty could be by itself.

Anton requested that they travel by way of Ensenada to San Felipe. He was bringing down some supplies for the house and probably would not have to pay duty in Tijuana, as he most surely would in Mexicali. Gary would ride with Anton in his van. Charlene followed with Josh in her well-stereoed and fashionable Porshe.

All crossed the border without incident, and headed down the toll road toward Ensenada. Gary noticed how along the way much of the construction he could see was incomplete. Anton said that ever since the economic trouble began in the early eighties it was hard to get things finished. He said, "Take my small development, for example, we can't get the power turned on because we paid for the job when the peso was worth about three times what it is now. Today, what we paid would be a steal, and no one really expects the power company to absorb that much of a loss."

Anton's attitude was stoical. "My boy, you've just got to realize that things are different down here. There's a Mexican way to get things done, and after awhile you even learn to appreciate how it all can work together just fine, though at first it's difficult to make sense of what they're doing."

About an hour and a half later after a spectacular ride along the coast that rivaled the famed Pacific Highway of Northern California they passed through a maze of streets in Ensenada, and headed inland across the long narrow finger of land that is Baja. The interior of the peninsula was rural, and quite beautiful. Gary thought how it must look like the old American West before it was overpopulated. Many ranchos were evidence of a variance in priority from the North with their modern satellite dishes for television standing beside their dilapidated buildings and outhouses.

Anton drove fast along the country road, and with his cassette of African pop music in the tape player Gary began to let the magical feel of being in a foreign land alter his view of the world enough so that he could be open to a new experience. And there is certainly a magic about Mexico.

What you would expect is not often what you find, and that, to Gary's mind, seemed exactly what he needed.

The road twisted and climbed as it crossed the mountains that rise up like a spine down the center of the land. To the west was the Pacific Ocean and once they reached the summit they would see the calm waters of the Sea of Cortez to the east. In the United States, this sea is called the Gulf of California, but since none of the large body of water touches the United States, Anton said it was wrong to call it by its gringo name.

"I'm always amazed," he said, "that Americans are able to ignore their southern neighbors so casually. When was the last time you saw an evening newscast in San Diego give the weather for Tijuana? Even though, most likely, more people live there than San Diego."

Gary didn't know what to say. He had never thought about it.

"I can't understand how they just ignore it, like the people here are of no importance. And it's the hard work, the "illegal" labor, of those good people that greases the machine of the so-called American dream."

Gary knew Anton, an opinionated intellectual, didn't really expect an answer. So he turned his attention out the window at the untamed countryside. There was no doubt he was not in America. Dips in the road were preceded by signs warning of danger from floods, and every so often overturned in these ravines would be the shell of a car decomposed over the years by thieves and nature. Mounds next to the highway would be topped by a small white cross dressed with fresh flowers in memory of someone who had died along the way. Gary thought of the settlers bury- ing their dead as they moved west across the trails of America, but then quickly realized his image was too romantic. In the U.S., no one wants to be reminded of how close death can be in a car, for the car is what made America great. In Mexico, though, the car is just a tool, and one that is too often the last to be used.

As they drove through a narrow gorge, Gary's idle reflection on trans- portation was abruptly ended by a man standing on the side of the road with a machine gun.

"Don't panic," said Anton in a calm voice. "It's just a Federal Check Point. They're looking for drugs and guns—mostly guns, but they will still harass us a little so we'll go back and tell our friends in the States how well the Mexican government is doing their part in the drug war."

"You mean it's just a front."

"No, it's more than that." He smiled maliciously, "They're pretty happy when they catch someone."

Gary was nervous. He had never been put in this position before, treated somewhat like a criminal, while just driving on vacation. A trailer was parked next to the road around which sat three or four plump Mexicans in plain clothes that were too tight against their sweaty oily skin. Off to the side, what looked like a group of Americans must have been caught with something. They looked restless. Up ahead on the road stood another man with a gun. Gary felt trapped, and almost thought he might be guilty of something.

Anton stopped the car and partially rolled down the window to talk to the officers.

"Buenos tardes, Señores," said the man standing in front, his breath foul enough for Gary to notice across the car. He was apparently the one in charge, though there was no way to know by his appearance, dressed extremely casual, in a short sleeve shirt unbuttoned to his belly.

Anton, forever patient, said in clear, proud, English, "Good Afternoon to you, Sir."

The agent was drinking something dark out of a large plastic cup. After taking a slow sip he said, "Do you have any drugs, or guns with you?"

"No."

"Where are you going?"

"San Felipe."

"Please step out of the car."

Anton got out quickly as ordered, still not worried. Though, getting out of the car made Gary really uncomfortable. A different agent asked him for his wallet. He removed the money from it and handed all of it to Gary. Then, he slowly examined what remained for evidence.

Gary tried to look innocent. Of course, he had used drugs and was afraid that somehow this would show through his demeanor. They would never find anything but it would be inconvenient to have them search through everything. The agent closed the wallet and handed it back. He then said something in Spanish to the other man talking to Anton.

Anton's interrogator did not respond at first, but then he asked for him to open the trunk. Gary felt his worst fear was to be realized. The trunk was stuffed with clothes and bags of personal belongings. It would be a mess if they went through everything, the facial scrubs, shampoos, condoms, and lube. But the agents just looked casually through the contents before they were satisfied to let them go.

And go they did, at least up to a turn-off in the road beyond the second machine gun, where they then pulled off to wait for Charlene and Josh to get through. They, fortunately, also had no difficulty, and the remainder of the trip passed without incident.

The fishing village of San Felipe sits tucked into the side of a volcanic cinder cone next to the turquoise waters of the Sea of Cortez. For its small size, it is bustling community being a resort for Mexicali to the North, Tijuana and Ensenada to the West, and a retreat for Americans looking for a place to party outside the country. The main streets are paved, but most roads are still dirt. Along picket fences children kick balls for fun while wild dogs forage for what small scraps of food can be found lying about. Old women in shanty stands built to shield them from the sun, heat up nearly black oil to fry fragments of fish for tacos. Men in groups stand sweat faced holding "turtle" sized bottles of beer getting drunk and laughing. American tourists act their worse, since they feel Mexican law has no jurisdiction over them. On weekends they drive up and down the beach with their dune buggies and all-terrain vehicles disrespectful of the peace and beauty with which nature has blessed the landscape. Mexican families come also to the shore and sit in the shade of unfinished construction, cook themselves dinner, and talk and enjoy life late into the night.

Anton was building himself a home on the beach at the south end of town. The local builders thought he was crazy wanting to live so far away from the village. Mexicans as a rule are a communal people. For Anton to live all alone by the sea without having been banished from society seemed peculiarly American. But no one refused to take his money to construct whatever he wanted, and slowly but surely his house took grand shape.

Since the hard economic times began a decade earlier only a few of the homes in his development had been completed, though some families had already set up housekeeping in the concrete and brick frames, usually in a part that was more finished. There was an advantage to not having final inspection by the State in that property tax was not levied until the building was certified complete. As a result, in Mexico, it should come as no surprise, very few buildings were ever completely finished.

Anton's home had stark white plaster walls with large Mexican pavers tiling the floors. The warm air made the space comfortable, instead of what would be considered cold in a cooler climate. The rooms had large windows that opened out onto the sea, and the smell of the breeze was like a sleeping potion to a newcomer. Anton's room was upstairs in what was supposed to be the den, the bedrooms were down a level. Charlene and Josh took the master bedroom with its large fireplace. Gary took the smaller room next to them and off the patio for himself.

Dropping his suitcase against the wall, Gary threw open the window and laid back on the bed. He was free of all obligation, and he tried to let his body catch up with this reality. His stomach was still anxious to do something, something not readily available to his mind to be known. He feared he would not begin to enjoy himself until this feeling was relieved.

Anton came into his room. "Want to go into town and get something for dinner?"

"Sounds good," said Gary.

"Maybe we could get some fresh fish to barbecue, and make fish tacos."

"Is that traditional?"

"No, locally they'd rather dip the fish in batter and fry it, but I think our way will be better. Less cholesterol, you know."

"I think Charlene and Josh are taking a nap," said Gary. "Guess the drive tired them out."

"No problem. We'll be back before they get up."

The ride to town was short. Anton stopped at the fish market to get two large fish, the sub-agencia to buy a case of beer, the water purification plant to get 40 liters of clean water, and last but not least, the liquor store to buy some tequila and margarita mix. It was a masterful shopping exercise, with them returning home in less than an hour. Charlene and Josh woke to the sound of the blender, and got up to toast Gary's birthday and their weekend of fun in the sun.

Anton toasted, "To you kids finally making it down."

"Kids," laughed Charlene. "I wish; every time I see a new wrinkle in the mirror."

Anton sipped his drink. "It's more than just wrinkles that makes me feel old. When you turn fifty you might begin to understand what I mean. It's like you step back out of society and become invisible. Once, my friends and I were the center of attention. Now, the young ones hardly notice us. We're on the edge, and it's hard watching you young folks bumble, because in our time we could be just as cruel."

"What are you talking about," said Josh. "You look great for your age, you have this beautiful place to live, and a good job. I hope I do as well."

"Materially I have a lot, it's true," said Anton. "But I'm not always happy…"

"I think I know what you mean," said Gary. "I was at the gym the other day when this guy I remembered from way back came in. He was part of the in-crowd then, and I remember looking up to him. I never did get to know him, but still he was one of the people that counted. When he came into the gym that day he looked old. I wondered if he was sick. But what struck me most was that when he signed in the register no one checked him out. People aren't that obvious at my gym, but you can tell when some young stud walks in how a lot of energy moves in their direction. I remember when this guy commanding that kind of energy. Now, he claimed nothing. It scared me a little."

"What?" asked Charlene looking disgusted that Gary would even fantasize that he was not longer attractive.

"It could be that I'm also getting old, but I think what really scares me is that I see too much."

"Or make too big a deal about nothing," added Josh.

"No one wants to think about getting old," said Anton. "We assume all that's good is young, while it's the young that are the most confused about what to value."

"I think there's a difference between confusion, and naivete," said Charlene.

"Yeah," added Josh. "I make mistakes all the time, but know that, and don't pretend to be better than I am."

Charlene smiled. "I guess that's why you get so upset when things don't go your way."

"I'll admit I have a temper," said Josh. "But you know I'm working on that."

"Oh, I'm not complaining." She gave her boyfriend a squeeze. "I think it's kinda sexy."

Gary too thought how Josh was very sexy when he was defending himself. He exuded masculinity in anger, but without any of the machismo which usually was an instant turn-off.

Gary interjected, "But you see what you guys are talking about is something totally different than what Anton and I are experiencing as we get older. You two have each other, and the culture is different for a strait couple anyway. Everything is set up to support you staying together, and not just because you look good together. Gay culture is not so well defined."

"I don't know," said Charlene. "Sounds like you have a romantic view of how things are for us. From what I've seen, nothing's really all that different."

Anton lit the charcoal barbeque on the balcony, while Charlene knifed away at the condiments. Gary, feeling a little lightheaded from a few margaritas, rested on the sofa. And Joshua, in typical fashion, had gone for a walk down the beach. Charlene looked across the room at Gary and remembered when they first came to San Diego eight years before.

She recalled a clear day in January, when the Santa Ana winds were blowing across the Southland. Sometimes these winds could be unbearably hot, but other times, that time in particular, they could bring the most spectacular of weather. In the dead of winter, the sky was sunny and crystal clear blue, with the air dry and warm. Charlene recalled how Gary's spirits, which had been depressed for some time, lightened, and how he had managed to convince her to move away from their life in St. Louis with just two weeks notice.

Then, Charlene was madly in love with Gary, though she would have never admitted it. When she was honest with herself, she still loved him now. He was such a sensitive man, if a little distant and unapproachable. No one ever seemed able to touch him. In fairness, he had always been honest with her about his being gay, and she had no hidden desire to change him into something different. He was so adorable, lonely, and in need of love. And he accepted her love and gave back more than she could have ever hoped for, more than she had ever received from any straight man.

When they had cause to sleep together she ached to make love to him. And for his part, he would move close to touch her soft and delicate skin. Trying to get aroused, nerves always frustrated him. He knew he needed to dominate her, to be aggressive, but he respected her too much for that. For her part, she respected him too much to act on her feelings and take advantage of him.

Every day after they moved was like a holiday. They would drink beer, smoke dope, and ride their bikes along the boardwalk, laughing and admiring the beautiful display of young tanned skin. The early Eighties were a sensual time in America anyway, and while the sexual revolution had not really made it any easier to have good sex, it had made it easier to tease, and Charlene couldn't help thinking, many times easier to get frustrated.

The big move had made everything possible for them. It was the first time in Charlene's life she ever took control of her destiny. Gary had been her inspiration. The world was something they could create for themselves, and anything seemed possible. She wondered how they had ever settled back down into the ruts they were now living.

Her life and Gary's had grown apart over the years. He had never confided in her, but recently she knew that he was again disheartened. His energy was the same as it had been before they moved. The worse part was that they both knew life could be so different. A line from a Talking Head's song had been the slogan for their first move. It seemed to apply just as well again. Everything was exactly the "same as it ever was."

In the Sixties Charlene was just one generation behind the baby-boomers coming of age. Those "older kids" always said that they would never trust anyone over thirty. Charlene was only nine, and when her mother turned thirty she did seemed to be some different kind of person and so much older. But when the baby-boomers started turning thirty, of course they changed their tune around to make being thirty-something the in-thing of the day.

Fortunately, Charlene had not made the mistake of youth to condemn age as something bad out-right, and consequently she was not bound to see it as something necessarily good either. When she turned thirty it felt natural to grow old. And for the first time in her life she began to relax and accept herself. She wished she could share some of that peace with her dear friend Gary.

"What'cha thinking about?" she asked across the room.

"I hope nothing," he answered with a nervous laugh. "It's been a while since I gave my mind a rest. I'd like to make the most of it."

"Remember when we moved to San Diego? That was sure a wonderful time."

"Yeah. I've been thinking about that a lot lately. I miss doing more with you."

"Well, you know how it is. A relationship takes time."

"You and Josh getting along pretty well?"

"Seems so. But do you ever really know?"

Gary sat up. "Charlene, I'm surprised at you. That doesn't sound like true love."

"Dear, I've been burned too many times to be romantically in love. We're doing fine, I guess. But I'd be lying to say everything was perfect."

"I wish the guys I met were more honest like you. They always pretend everything is great until one day by chance you see them out alone on the prowl, and the dreamboat's all of a sudden an asshole."

"Why does that bother you? It's the way of the world."

"Because it makes me feel like something's wrong with me for being single. If all love is pretend, I'd rather stay out of love and have a few good friends that I really care about."

"I don't think Josh and I are pretending to be in love..."

"I wasn't talking about you."

"Although, I must admit, sometimes he does seem peculiar and distant."

Just then Anton walked in and announced, "The coals look ready."

"Great! I'm starved," said Gary.

"It won't be long now," said Anton as he grabbed the fish off the counter. "Where's Josh, Charlene?"

"Out walking I think, but he knows we're going to eat. He'll be back soon enough when he's sure there's no more work to be done."

Anton smiled, "Then I hope he likes doing dishes, because dinner's not free to anyone."

And it was true, Josh did return just in time to eat.

The others were finishing their second margarita, and began blending one for Josh to catch up. The fish, wrapped in aluminum foil was steaming on the grill next to some fresh corn on the cob. Charlene placed the small bowls of condiments she had prepared onto the counter. There was a fresh salsa, some guacamole, a dish of chopped cilantro, one of fresh tomato, and some lime wedges. Gary looked unsuccessfully in the cupboards for the paper plates until he stopped to pour Josh his drink out of the blender.

"Have a good walk?" he asked.

"Yep," Josh answered without much feeling.

It frustrated Gary that he couldn't get to know this man better. After all, he was the other half of his best friend, and while that might not be grounds for a good friendship in itself, at least, Gary hoped it might be grounds for more than cordiality. To provoke Josh into conversation he asked as he handed him a drink, "See anything?"

"It's really dirty out there."

Gary looked out the window at the white beach with its long tidal slope into the deep blue water of the sea. The town sat off in the distance around the gentle curve of the bay. The clouds were just beginning to show the spectacular color of sunset. And in spite of this scene, Josh could only see it as dirty because of some trash scattered about.

Gary protested, "Dirty? Josh, look out the window, it's a beautiful sunset."

"Oh, sure," Josh conceded. "The sunset's pretty enough. I mean on the beach. All the construction shit just lying around. Trash everywhere. Don't these people have any pride about how they live?"

Anton walking over answered, "They have less pride about and more enjoyment in life. That's what I admire."

Josh shook his head in disgust, "I don't see how they can have any enjoyment living like pigs."

Charlene scolded, "Josh." She hated when he was so pig-headed himself. Even though Anton and Gary were far from being offended by her friend she rather avoid any discomfort because of his behavior.

Josh flashed her a look of contempt. She was not his mother, and he would damn well say whatever he pleased. Yet, to keep the peace, he toned down his disgust with the poverty around him. He answered Anton, "Well, I guess it would be fun cooking dinner on the beach."

"It's tradition," said Anton.

"Hey," Josh changed the subject. "I walked down to that small harbor. What kind of fishing do they do here."

Anton answered, "The sea is rich. When it's in season, those are shrimpers."

"I thought I saw one out a ways."

"Probably did. It's Saturday. No inspectors on duty, so no one to stop them. It's the way here."

Josh just shook his head. He thought, Mexicans. "You mean, just because the law's off duty, sitting in town, probably getting drunk, they go out and fish illegally and no one says anything."

"Most likely they pay the inspector off."

"Crazy culture," said Josh.

Gary interjected, "In the U.S. they do the same thing, only not so obviously."

"That's because," said Josh, "in the States there's a respect for order."

"You mean, the appearance of order," said Anton. "Just as much crime goes on there, people are just more careful to cover it up."

Men, thought Charlene. They are always posturing to outmaneuver each other, or was it out-manure. She grabbed the blender and walked around filling each of their glasses. The woman's role, she thought with a little frustration. But how could she say the conversation was bullshit, that would be a woman's role too, and she wanted to fit in more than confront.

The silence was obvious and awkward. Anton finally broke it by saying, "Gary, why don't you put on one of your tapes."

"Which one?" he asked. Having to choose music made him nervous. His taste in music was not always popular. There was one time he made a tape especially for the gym where he worked out thinking it would be nice to have a more eclectic mix of music for those members who would appreciate it. When he had the morning instructor play it, by the third song of a ninety minute cassette someone came up to complain that the music sounded communistic, and asked for it to be turned off. Communistic, pondered Gary: of all the ways to criticize a collection of songs, especially by someone who would have it turned off. Of course, the song that inspired the complaint was Cabaret Voltaire's "Thank You America," which does end with the refrain, "We don't believe in no God. We don't believe in no Jesus. We don't believe in no Bible." A double negative, thought Gary amused, that just sounds revolutionary.

"How about that tape of country music."

"You mean the one with the Residents "Buckaroo Blues"?"

"Yeah."

The Residents, of course, were not normally thought of as a country music band, but this piece of their's was more evocative of the West to Gary's ear than most songs that were supposed to be more authentic. He had taped it along with some other country songs he liked, as well as an environmental piece by Steve Roach and some African dance music he knew Anton appreciated. It was great dinner music. And Anton enjoyed its difference, while Charlene enjoyed it as something uniquely Gary, and Josh thought is was weird, but peer pressure prevented him from saying anything but a awkward compliment out-loud.

Anton, feeling content with the music, his company, and the numbing buzz of his margarita said, "After we eat I think we should go into town. This is the last weekend of the season…and it should be wild out."

ACROSS THE BORDER

While they were cleaning up after dinner, Tony asked, "Anyone want to get stoned?"

And the faces of his guests became animated with mixed signs of pleasure, disbelief, and shock.

"You brought stuff down with you through the checkpoint?" one asked.

"I can't believe it," said another.

But Tony was calm. "No way," he answered in a husky giggle to mock their concern. "It's easy enough to get dope down here. There's no need to risk getting caught bringing it."

"But I thought," said Charlene, "that the Mexicans were making a real effort to stop drug smuggling."

"They are," said Tony, "but there are people down here like in the U.S. that want to smoke, and will pay for it, so there's always someone that'll make it available. A fine example of the Capitalist spirit, if you ask me. One that should ease the Conservative worry that our next-door-neighbor might not be Red, White, and Blue enough."

Choosing to avoid Tony's obvious provocation to an argument, Gary moved the group out of trouble. He said, "Sure, Tony, I'll smoke with you."

"Great!" returned the host, who began a ritual for loading his pipe. After reaching for a lighter off the coffee table he lit the pipe and took a long drag, then passed it over to Gary. Charlene and Josh moved to sit closer, in two chairs made of leather and sticks that looked uncomfortable,

but surprisingly were not, and at the same time were the epitome of glossy
home magazine fashion.

The marijuana shifted Gary's perception almost immediately. To the
east, beyond the mountains the sun had finished its hard day of work, the
air cooled, and the stars began to take their places in the night sky. Across
the calm water of the bay, fireworks were shot off by people in celebration
of nothing special. But the next day was Gary's birthday, and he imagined
somewhat immaturely that every display was especially for him.

Dope can do that for a small person. It can make them feel like the
immediate center of the universe, and in such a heightened state of awareness any thought tends to become profound. Gary, sober, thought of himself as special, and now the idea of his importance seemed like a wonderful
insight, even if the next day it might sound rather silly. He, fortunately,
had kept the insight to himself, and was later glad that he did.

Charlene, Josh, and Tony, were laughing about a cocktail party they
had all attended as part of Charlene's job as the Society reporter for the
morning edition of the paper. Gary was glad they were ignoring him
because he felt like the look on his face was one of sadness. Yet he wasn't
so sad, despite that quite often his reflections on life had a sobering quality about them. Normally, someone pretending to be happy would complain that he was too serious, but these friends present knew better than
to comment like that. He never was all that serious, just reserved to
becoming another babbling idiot of the crowd.

Gary recalled the party as well. It took place at the Timkin Art Museum
in Balboa Park, where he had the good fortune to work as a janitor and be
well paid to maintain a clean space for art. The Mayor had just announced
his plan to have a Chinese Art Festival as part of a publicity campaign
designed to boost his personal image as the cultured leader of America's
seventh largest city, whose name might better be Provençal, unless, of
course, there was some connection between culture and a quick way to
make money.

Charlene always complained it was unfair to criticize San Diego for its lack of taste. After all, the average person was never exposed to any art worth supporting. Anything happening was happening in L.A., or New York. Nothing, of intellectual or visceral interest, could ever spring up from the sun baked shores of the Southern wasteland of bathing beauties and bad surfers, never-mind that the climate of the Mediterranean is much the same. Art to the modern critic must ooze from the darkest depths of despair, and a nice view makes it hard to always look at life in that light. Besides, more than one work of art has been inspired by young, tanned, flesh.

Flesh like that of Josh, which if his name had been David might have easily inspired the likes of Michelangelo. The direction of Gary's reflection surprised him. He had never before consciously thought of Josh in a sexual, he meant artistic way, yet watching Charlene's lover enjoying himself with the others aroused an erotic desire in Gary. Out of respect for his old girlfriend he quickly suppressed it, though not before taking notice of the fantasy. Josh was a good-looking man, and Gary was happy that Charlene had found such a companion.

"Remember when the Mayor got up on Giovanni's Mercury," said Charlene. "I thought I'd die when he grabbed the statue's leg for support and his hand almost touched its little dick. The director looked mortified, and it was all I could do to resist headlining my article "MAYOR SHOWS LOVE OF ART BY FONDLING STATUE."

"He didn't really do that?" objected Tony in disbelief.

"I swear," said Charlene. "Ask Gary. He was there."

"Yeah," said Gary reluctantly returning to the group giving up his aloofness. "He didn't really grab the statue, but it was pretty amazing that he even stood up on its marble pedestal."

"I should say," said Tony. "It's frightening when politicians try to lead the electorate."

"Well, I got a good laugh out of it," said Charlene. "Even if my story turned out boring. My editor says he only wants the facts, but really means fiction. He's a friend of the Mayor, you know."

From over the crashing surf a steady base beat was heard by all. Josh asked, "Where's the music coming from?"

Tony replied, "See that neon across the bay. That's Rockadile, a new bar in town. I couldn't believe the sound could travel this far until I saw the speakers they have set up outside. One of the big discos in TJ built it for the college kids that come down here on holiday."

"Sounds like it's hopping," said Charlene.

Tony asked, "Let's go into town for a while? We can get a drink to celebrate Gary's birthday."

Everyone agreed, but the trouble they had getting up revealed that they were already celebrating. Finally making it out the door, they decided to take Charlene's car which was parked closest to the front of the house. She got it started, and the stereo pulsed the beat of U2's new album, a rocking sound with just the right amount of an inspired production flare to add a mystical quality to the night drive. Tony sat up in front with her. Josh and Gary squeezed next to each other in the back seat.

While the town was always the same distance from Tony's house, making the trip that particular evening was a very different experience than making the same trip by daylight. The absence of street lamps, and the glare of oncoming traffic, combined with the Mexican tradition of placing huge speed bumps across the road without any warning, made for a ride that might have scared Mr. Toad. Everyone was trusting Charlene, and to her credit she was driving very well.

Arriving in town they found it packed with people as expected. Most of them were Mexican, with quite a few college students, and a fair share of Zoners, the Californian name for a suburban class of people from Arizona who were defined by their bad manners and need to ride all-terrain-vehicles. A hot day in the sun made most everyone look sweaty and sunburned. Charlene parked the car next to a rickety fence on a dirt side road just down the street from what seemed to be some kind of a carnival. A loudspeaker energetically announced something that sounded like it was exciting in Spanish.

Unfortunately, no one in the group spoke Spanish well enough to make sense of what the loudspeaker was saying. It sounded like a call of some kind, perhaps to fun. But what was fun was hard to tell, considering the circus consisted of a dilapidated travel trailer and yellow tent. In front of the trailer hung a canvas drop showing animal acts and children playing gleefully. Several people stood around the shadows of a solitary light bulb illuminating the scene. They stood by a rope that was hanging in front of the tent. They were waiting. But nothing seemed to be happening.

After a moment, though not one too long, because even though the dope distorted time for the group, this all happened as they walked past the circus toward the main street of town, a lone, scrawny, Rhesus monkey came slowly from inside the tent and walked over to the rope and began playing on it timidly. Gary thought, something is wrong here. Could this poor animal really be a whole circus? The others didn't seem to notice.

As for the Mexican audience, it stood mesmerized by the animal's antics. Off to the side of the scene, children threw small stones into ashtrays in order to win tacky papier-mache prizes. Next to them an old Indian woman fried fish in a well-used skillet to sell to the tourists inside handmade corn tortillas.

There, less than three hundred miles from home, Gary had entered into another world. Instead of disgusting or frightening him, like it did many Americans, for the first time in years Gary felt the wonder of life like a child. He was waking up, because the world was different than he expected and he was not able to pretend he knew what it was all about and become bored.

"Rockadile's just around the corner," said Tony. "I've never seen this place so crowded."

"Look at that line," exclaimed Charlene. "It goes half way around the block."

"Hey, Gar," said Josh as he nudged Gary. "There's one for you."

Indeed, walking down the street with his girlfriend was a young college student, muscular, without an ounce of fat, and eyes that could bring a man or woman to their knees. Charlene was unable to control herself and whistled at him. The boy cracked back a slight smile of gratitude to the obvious displeasure of his date. Gary was embarrassed by Charlene, even though he would have like to do the same thing.

"What a hunk!" said Charlene. "I think I like it here."

Josh gave her a spank on the ass and scolded, "You better behave yourself. You know how you get when you drink."

"How do I get?…Lover boy."

"You know. You get loose."

She stroked his face. "That never bothered you before. I thought you kind of liked it when I got a little wild."

"A little, maybe. Sometimes you go too far."

"Joshua Juduson, you're one to talk. What about the time when you were too drunk to notice, I fell off your bike when you pulled out of the parking lot like a madman."

"I wasn't too drunk to notice. I was trying to ditch you. As I recall, you had just insulted my manliness."

Charlene, loving the playful antagonism of the exchange, assaulted, "Saying you don't have the biggest dick I've ever seen is not an insult. It happens to be the truth."

Gary had always thought Josh filled a pair of pants rather nicely. He wondered what made him insecure.

"All right, Charlene," said Josh in a sterner parental tone of voice.

"Trying to pull in the reigns, big boy?"

"It's no use, Josh," said Gary knowing Charlene the longer of the two. "When she gets like this, she's incorrigible."

To the side, Josh, agreed and added, "Worse than that, she's…so…fuckn' sexy at the same time."

The two men laughed, and of course Charlene assumed they were making fun of her.

Finally making it inside the bar they found it packed with bronzed sweaty flesh, now mostly American, acting like they were at a Saturnalia. Our gang of four felt a little uncomfortable fitting in until Tony quickly eased their nerves by buying a round of Volcanos, Pina Coladas with a floater of Bacardi 151. Relaxed after the first stiff sniff, they found themselves a place to stand and settled down to have a good time. Four drinks later they were bombed.

Josh was standing next to Gary, and it seemed he was pressing closer than was normally proper. Gary would move his body in a gentle caress of Josh's strong arm, which seemed to respond with reciprocation of every advance. All the while Josh talked loudly with Charlene and Tony, he conspicuously avoided speaking to Gary directly. The contradiction of his actions was a turn-on to Gary who found his tactics erotically subversive.

Charlene, who appeared the most smashed of all, alternated between hanging on Josh and Gary. She really loved them both, but it was seldom that she felt so uninhibited to make such a public display of affection. Josh had long ceased being jealous of Gary. It was clear Charlene would always love her friend from the past. Gary, after all, had saved her from a mundane life as a sales rep for an electronics company. She had good and bad experiences since those days, but not one day had she been so bored, and many nights she would thank Gary in her prayers for his courage, or foolhardiness, that had forced her to quit her job on short notice and make the switch to create adventure.

"I'm the luckiest girl in the world," she said as she sensuously stroked the now bare chests of her two dear men.

Even though it was late in the evening, it was still hot in the bar and many people had stripped down their clothing with the pretext of staying cool but the real motive of exotic bird-like displays for attention. Josh's strong and hairy chest looked edible, and Tony watched with a smile when Charlene in an infrequent lapse of ladylike etiquette took a healthy nibble of his right tit. Gary, catching Tony in the act of voyeurism, through a glance of "behave yourself," united the two gay men in an understanding that Josh did indeed look good enough to eat.

Sometimes it was hard for men like Tony and Gary to mingle in the strait world. Other times it was great fun stalking that foreign land. In a gay bar, the eroticism of the situation would be totally lost in the acceptability of men touching and watching other men together. But in a "straight" bar it was not part of the scene for men to be watching another man get turned on by a woman, although Gary was aware of others taking equal delight in the display. A strange world, he thought, that makes so many rules about proper behavior which no one has any desire to live up to at all.

"I saw one of those bronco machines outside," said Tony. "Wonder which of you two studs could ride it the longest?"

"There's no doubt," said Josh. "I was raised on a horse."

Gary countered, "Don't be so sure, I've ridden a few horses in my day."

Charlene, hysterical over Gary's comeback, said, "I bet you have, cowboy. I'd sure like to see which of you could ride it longer."

"There's a challenge boys," said Tony. "I think we should satisfy our lady's curiosity."

It took a while to work their way out of the bar because of the crowds trying to buy drinks, and the fact that they were already loaded and not often focused. Even though it was after midnight the air outside remained balmy with many people still walking up and down the boardwalks of the town. A crowd stood in front of a Mexican Ice Cream parlor, and beyond them, up on a hill, stood the bronco busting machine. Spectators circled the machine which had bags of dirt all around it in order to "cushion" the fall. Given the condition of most people riding the machine, they could have fallen on concrete and probably not felt it until the next day.

Anyone who walked out to ride became an instant celebrity to the spectators looking for a vicarious thrill. As Gary and Josh moved toward the Que a girl was preparing to mount the beast after her boyfriend had just dazzled everyone with a long ride and remarkable fall that concluded with a thud that went all the way to the gut of everyone watching. The operator, who controlled the beast manually, gave her a slow ride to start, the audience letting out hoots and hollers of emotion as the metal animal moved in slow circles at first, then faster with a bolt. The ride was cautious, though before too long it got wild enough to throw the girl down to the ground.

Gary was the first of the boys to ride. He walked out to the beast. Shirtless in his 501 jeans he looked good, and even though he was too drunk to tell exactly where any sound came from, he was made proud by the gasps of respect his strong body drew from those watching. Charlene, excited, stood next to Tony anxious to see how long Gary would be able to hold on.

The operator started him out slow, but since he was such a strong, proud, man he became quickly merciless with his mechanical assault against the drunk gringo. For the first few bolts Gary managed to maintain at least a semblance of control. But after one good 360-degree swing of the beast, Gary was hanging on for his life and he looked like it too. The crowd went wild with cheers of support and laughter over the comical positions Gary found himself swung into. He held on for quite awhile until finally the invisible force of the spin pulled him off the machine.

Flying through the air, Gary felt remarkably comfortable. He was out of control and the sound of the crowd mixed with the high alcohol content of his blood placed him in a protective cocoon of serenity, much like he might have imagined it felt in the womb. But when he hit hard on the bags of dirt, there was no doubt that the ride was over and his emotions joined his body lying flat on his back on solid ground.

Josh then walked out onto the bags of dirt even while Gary still lay there stunned from his fall. Standing over him, he feigned masturbating onto his buddy in a display of domination which delighted the audience and even in his drunken stupor exited Gary with its suggestion. Josh was also quite drunk. It would be wrong to assume any conscious motive to his actions. But Gary thought, while he looked up from the ground into his buddy's big blue eyes, that there was some kind of longing inside his friend trying to express itself in a world that had no ears to hear such a faint call.

Then Gary heard an odd cry of his own, from beyond the image of his friend or his location in space. It was like the wind blowing inside his head, unseen by others, yet whispering something for him to hear. An unpleasant pain shooting behind his eyes accompanied the sensation. Somehow he knew it was necessary for the experience. The wind blew a word, but Gary wasn't sure of the language, or its meaning. A peace descended onto him, a peace like being at home, or of welcome.

Perhaps this impression alone was the meaning, he wondered. But then, as quickly as the noise had come to him, the sound and discomfort vanished revealing an image before him of a lonely old woman sitting in a simple wooden chair at a small card table within a pale green room. Gary saw her as if peeking through a window. She was ancient, and sat with her hands before her in stillness. Her eyes gazed ahead into space as if she saw the dark time of her end approaching. She sat waiting. Beyond her room, the bright lights of the city bustled with the traffic of a Saturday night, young people got drunk, fell in love, and pretended they would never die. The woman turned her glance at Gary. She saw him, and smiled.

Gary passed out. The next thing he remembered was waking up on his bed back at the house. Still disoriented from the liquor and marijuana, it took him a moment to recall that he had gone out with his friends and that they must have brought him back home, undressed him, and put him to bed. The room was spinning. He closed his eyes and thought he would surely vomit, but rolling onto his side he finally settled down to an uneasy sleep.

Josh never rode the bronco machine. When he saw his buddy pass out his first fear was that the throw had somehow injured him. Josh was young. In his twenty-six years he never knew the death of someone close to him. He shuddered to think that this time of fun would be his rude initiation into the hard reality of life's meaning. Reaching down to Gary he could feel him breathing, and only then did Josh move back to his present and pick up his friend. The night was over. They all had fun, but when one was down the others couldn't be far behind, and everyone knew it was time to go home.

Josh carried Gary downstairs to his room and took off his clothes. He was still pretty loaded and it seemed like getting off each shoe took forever. And Gary's pants were so tight they could barely be peeled off. It was then Josh's hands first brushed against Gary's still sweaty thigh. The strength of his friends leg was intriguing. His hand lingered awhile, to gently rub against the soft hair covering them. Tucking Gary under his sheet, Josh nervously retired to his own room.

Charlene had passed out on the bed wearing only her skimpy lace briefs. Josh admired her body illuminated by the flattering light of the moon. A breeze blew into the room off the sea. It was cool, and salty. The sound of the waves gently lapping made the room seem like paradise. Josh undressed. Lying on his back he was wide awake. The alcohol had worn off a bit leaving him still stoned, but wired. And all he could think about was Gary.

Slowly at first, his hand moved across his body. Every inch was sensitive and alive to the touch. He rubbed his legs and felt his own soft hair beneath his fingers. He began to rub his crotch and quickly became aroused. Fantasy images filled his mind. He tried to think of Charlene and having sex with her, remembering some of his favorite times they had been together. But when he would become the most excited his mind would wander, and he was more than surprised to see before him the image of Gary.

He thought of the times Charlene, Gary, and he would be together, cutting up with each other. These were good times, but hardly sexual. Then a feeling would rise up inside him, a feeling that his masturbation intensified. It was a strong feeling toward Gary. Different from the love he felt for Charlene, but similar. His love for Charlene was tender. This feeling for

Gary was hard and driven. He wanted to be with Gary, to have him as a companion. Not necessarily for sex, but a presence is sexual, and he wanted Gary to be close.

Josh thought of his friend at the beach, playing hard in the strong surf of the sea. Gary would be so happy when he would catch a big wave for a long ride. He would jump up out of the ocean waving his muscular arms, his body glistening in the hot sun. Joshua focused on his arms. Then, he focused on his chest. Then…

Stopping for a moment, Josh looked to see if Charlene was sound asleep. She was. He carefully got up out of bed and walked to the bath-room. He had to piss badly, and in order to get full satisfaction from his play he needed to relieve himself. On the way back to his room he stopped in front of Gary's door. Peeking in, he saw Gary asleep on his side. Josh stepped into the doorway and began playing with himself as he looked at his friend. The fact that what he was doing was out of character and for-bidden made it all the more exciting. He walked slowly over to Gary's bed, always afraid that Gary would wake up to see him, and at the same time always hoping that he would.

Gary stirred.

Josh stopped, and moved quietly for the door. Looking back, he realized Gary was still asleep and so he worked his way slowly back to his bed. But Gary, who remained quite drunk and had not slept soundly for a second, was aware that someone was in his room. First, he thought it was Tony. And while he liked Tony, he was uncomfortable with him coming into his room so sneakily.

Gary believed that while it is true that sometimes you must push in order to get something you want, you should do that pushing in such a way that the other person has a graceful way to avoid your advance. What attracts any two people was a mystery to him. Most likely, it had something to do with karma, or something equally fantastic, nothing else made any sense, because the two people who should get together never seem to have the spark, while everywhere you look the most disparate kindling gets the fire going every time. No, he would rather not have to tell Tony he was not interested, so he feigned sleep in the hope that nothing would happen.

But Josh stayed in the room, standing in front of the doorway backlit by the night light in the hall. When Gary opened his eyes far enough to see the strong silhouette of his girlfriend's lover, he wasn't sure what to do. Was it a dream? He had hoped to be with Josh, but never even in his most erotic fantasy did he think he would have the chance in real life. But now there before him, while he was still swooning from too much to drink, stood his idol of straight masculinity playing with himself, if his eyes were to be believed. Gary became hard in an instant.

"Josh," Gary whispered. "Is that you?"

Josh froze. He was embarrassed.

"Come here," said Gary, in a soothing voice as he lifted his sheet so Josh could climb into bed next to him.

Josh hesitated, but the offer was inviting and, after all, it was why he had come there. Lying next to his friend he said with a tremble, "I don't know what to do."

Gary answered, "Don't you worry. I do."

The next morning Gary woke up alone, as he had expected. Josh had seemed to enjoy himself. And Gary had made the encounter one of tenderness, rather than lust. Sometime during the night Josh had gone back to Charlene, which after all was his rightful place. Gary knew this, but had mixed feelings. Besides having a splitting headache and hangover, he felt more alone than normal, and also the feeling that a part of himself was missing. It was like an invisible cord connected him to Josh and he wondered if Josh was feeling the same. Hollow might be one way to describe it, and if he wasn't so glad to have had the experience he would have cursed himself for placing himself in such a predicament.

He walked upstairs to get some coffee. Josh already had it made. He sat drinking a cup on the balcony looking out over the sea. The sun had just come up over the horizon and made a spectacular picture as its orange and white light mixed with the wispy clouds in the eastern sky.

"Morning, Josh."

With a big smile Josh returned, "Good morning, Gary."

Gary was relieved to see him in a good mood. Once before he had a straight buddy that manipulated him to fool around. After the fact his friend flipped out and would hardly speak to Gary. He had been the one to initiate the experience because of his curiosity, but he was unable to handle the consequence that he might not enjoy it, or that he might feel guilty. Gary, for the most part, was secure with himself. He really did not like being gay all that much, but had long come to the realization that it was something he was going to have to deal with if he was to live a genuine life. His friend saw Gary as the cause of his weakness, not his own incontinence. As a result, every time he looked at Gary he winced with pain, like he was already burning in Hell. This scarred Gary.

But now Josh smiled at him, which made him feel good, sort of. He would have felt better if he knew where it would all lead. He figured it had been fun for one night, might as well leave it at that. But he wanted to talk with Josh, share a bit of his life, and do more together. If they weren't able to do this, it would have been just a whore's trick. Gary would then feel used, and while he appreciated having the chance to experience his friend sexually, he would rather it had not happened if it was to be just a one night stand.

Gary asked, "You okay?"

"Yeah. But there's something I want to say to you."

Here it comes, thought Gary. Rejection again.

Josh said, "If I seem distant today, it's because I'm not sure what I'm feeling. But I know I want to see you again. I've never felt like you made me feel last night."

Ready for rejection, Gary startled to the realization that he might have received what he hoped for, and wondered if he could handle it.

THE VIRUS KILLS

*L*ater that afternoon the boys and Charlene thanked Tony for letting them come to visit, and under a blazing midday sun the group began the long trip home. Tony would stay in Mexico for a while taking care of some unfinished business relating to the construction of his house. Gary hated pretending that he had not been intimate with Josh, but Josh was quite convincing acting like nothing had happened. Charlene and he played their lover way. And Gary's suffering was double-edged since he also felt guilt about the possibility of hurting Charlene. She was obviously very much in love with Josh. And he thought it would be a terrible strain on their friendship if she ever discovered his unfaithfulness to her.

Josh drove the car. Charlene sat in front next to him, which left Gary to feel outcast sitting alone in the back seat. That was okay with him. Charlene had a great stereo in her car which sounded great from the back seat. She turned on the Cure's "Disappointed" cassette, and Gary's mood immediately tuned in with that album's moody pop sensuality. The music was deeply sad, but for some reason getting in touch with that sadness made him feel better than if he had no outlet for his emptiness and had to keep his feelings in complete denial.

Many of the lyrics were about death, a reality everyone must eventually face, and the fear of which makes most people do some very crazy things, the worst of which, thought Gary, is the wasting of time in keeping busy to avoid thinking about the grim reality of living. Sometimes, when a song makes death the focus of attention, it helps the soul live a more authentic life. Dealing with death directly is too painful to mean much for how to live, though it cannot be denied that when death comes close, life does seem more real. The Cure's music was just that kind of art. More than once Gary's eyes swelled up in appreciation of the bands talent.

When they reached the turn off to Ensenada, they decided to go straight through to Mexicali on the way home. Now the road entered a wasteland that was hostile and at the same time supremely sublime. The road rose up onto a causeway, and as far as the eye could see was a hot, cracked earth, desert. To the left, three spectacular dust devils slowly danced around each other toward the East. From inside the comfort of the air-conditioned car, with its stereophonic soundtrack, Gary felt like he was watching a New Age Video. His mind then easily slipped into a meandering meditation.

Since it had just been his birthday, he began his reflection with his age. Turning thirty should be no big deal, he thought. After all, it's not like anything happens over night. All of his life people had told Gary that he acted mature for his age. Now, he was mature, and he wondered if he shouldn't have let loose a little more while he was young.

Maybe he would have been more likely to enjoy himself if he wasn't such a Scientist. Always experimenting with the world, he would impassively watch the behavior of other people and mentally record the effect of their actions on their lives. Soon, he discovered that while for short periods of time people could genuinely have fun, in the long run, it almost always happened that they hid misery in their hearts. Their foolhardiness was great for making superficial friends, but when they needed a real friend, they were often alone, except for good old reliable Gary. Good old reliable Gary, who was little fun to play with, but someone to count on in times of need.

That kind of reliability is supposed to be a prize of value. Why then, Gary wondered, did being a good person make him feel so lonely? If only he could be one of the fun people for a change. Then, he paused, and had to laugh at himself. A fun person, no doubt, would never worry so much.

It was his worrying that lent a doomed quality to his personality. It was a lifetime of practice at worry that had turned that quality into stone.

There was about an hour's wait to cross the border. It was hot outside. Small children jumped on the car and began cleaning the windows for spare change. Later, they would demand payment for the job already done. It was the last contact with a different culture. An invisible line across the land kept separate. Across the border, in the United States of America, the world would be much different. The roads there are broad, and everything is neat, clean, and very expensive.

Charlene and Josh dropped Gary off in front of his house. Giving her long time friend a big kiss, Charlene said she hoped he'd had a good time. Josh, in turn, said a more masculine farewell, but his eyes said that he too hoped Gary had fun. Grabbing his bag out of the trunk, Gary waved to his two friends. His stomach felt uneasy, like he just got off a roller coaster. Joshua disoriented him. He wanted to spend more time alone with his new "friend," but knew there was no time for visiting today. Josh, like anyone worth anything, had plenty of life of his own.

The five-hour drive was exhausting. Walking into his house Gary first checked his answering machine. One message. It was from his friend Little John. A gym buddy named Joe was very sick with pneumonia and in the hospital. Only the week before Joe had talked with Gary. He had said he wasn't feeling very good. But pneumonia, thought Gary. Pneumonia.

Was it A.I.D.S.? Joe had been uncomfortable for the last few months. He said it was nerves. One time, Gary asked him point blank if he was all right, meaning had he been to a doctor to see if he had even been exposed to HIV. Joe assured him that his doctor could find nothing wrong with him, but that he kept having diarrhea. They thought it might be colitis. Joe was unhappy with his job as a flight attendant, and the stress of that unhappiness, they decided, could easily be making him sick.

Gary asked Joe if he had ever been tested for the virus. Joe honestly said he was too afraid. Gary understood, but said that it was wrong to seek medical help with half the facts. Did Joe's doctor even know that he was gay? No, said Joe. The doctor was his uncle, and his family, strict Catholic, and of Hispanic descent, would not understand his homosexuality.

Joe was twenty-eight years old, barely beyond a child. Now, he was sick enough to be in the hospital, and soon everyone would know he was gay anyway, and have to deal with it, but probably without much time to show him any love and support. And certainly no time to receive back a good life of accepting one another. They would stand by his bed, but that was the duty of any good Christian, not the unconditional love of the Christ. Joe's greatest fear, that his family would be shamed, was to be realized as his last experience on Earth.

Little John said that Joe had gone to his father's house on the weekend. He had been running a high temperature but kept saying it was just the flu. When his father checked on him Saturday night, he found his son unable to breathe, and unconscious. The paramedics struggled hard to keep him alive, and one of the emergency room attendants had told Little John that he truly thought Joe would not survive the night, but through heroic effort the hospital staff had pulled him through. Now, only one question remained, for what?

Gary took a shower, brushed his teeth, and headed up to the hospital. He was tired, but there might not be time for him to rest and still see his buddy outside of a coffin.

Joe was someone he knew from the gym. They never dated, and never had sex, even though Joe would always tease Gary, and for Gary's part he was at least interested initially. In time they had become close friends, seeing each other every day without the strain of an official relationship. They liked each other a lot, and would enjoy sharing time together. Now, one of their life's turned tragic, and Gary wanted to be close. The need for him was more than mere duty. Gary felt a part of himself in need of help.

Since Joe's family didn't know that he was gay, when they came to his aid they did not realize that they placed him not only into the different world of the hospital, but also into a different world of support. Of his gay friends only Little John was called because he alone had left a message on

Joe's answering machine with a phone number. Joe was glad his family had not abandoned him. And once he was aware of his condition he assumed everyone must know his story. He felt ashamed. But the truth was, they didn't know, or weren't willing to accept their son being gay as a possibility. No one ever mentioned his illness, and everyone talked hopefully of the day he would recover.

When Gary arrived at the hospital, he stood in a long line to ask the receptionist for Joe's room number. She checked her computer and said he was on the Seventh floor. Near the top of the building, thought Gary. Once before, early on, when the disease had yet to be named, he had visited a buddy who was dying of A.I.D.S.. He, too, was on the top floor with the other terminal patients, nearer heaven Gary supposed. Joe had a room to himself, which seemed, to those who were unaware, like a luxury for someone with a severe case of pneumonia.

Gary, timidly, stood in the door way. Joe's mother was spoon feeding her adult son. She didn't know Gary, but was glad to see Joe's smile of recognition from beneath his oxygen mask. He could barely breathe.

"Gary," Joe managed to strain out with a herculean effort. "How did you find out?"

"Little John called me."

It was awkward to talk. The effort was considerately greater for Joe, and Gary did not know what he could say around Joe's mother. She seemed to recognize the two men's uneasiness and, since she had been there all afternoon, decided to take the opportunity of Gary's visit to leave and take a break.

"I'll leave you two alone for a while," she said. "Joey, is there anything I can get you from outside?"

Taking the mask from his face so he could speak a little clearer, Joe answered, "An ice cream bar would be nice."

His mother smiled broadly. She wanted to do anything to ease the suffering of her son. "You bet."

Normally, an interest in such food would be a sign of recovery.

Gary sat next to Joe, who in some ways looked like he was already dead and in hell. He had lost about twenty pounds since Gary had last seen him only a few weeks before. His hair was matted, and the dark circles around his eyes, which before had been alluring and sexy, now, made his face look like a skull. His breathing was labored as an IV dripped nourishment he was unable to get from eating real food into his blood.

"So," said Gary trying to create the appearance that had absolutely nothing to do with how he felt. Joe was obviously very sick, and his condition, one in which Gary could see himself, frightened Gary. "What happened?"

"I thought I was sick with the flu, that's all," said Joe. "I went to my father's because I was running a high temperature. Next thing I knew, I was in intensive care."

"Little John said you have pneumonia. Is it pneumocystis?"

"I don't know. No one has said."

"Didn't you ask?" said Gary surprised.

"Come on…I'm twenty-eight years old, single, a flight attendant, with a case of pneumonia that almost killed me. What do you think?"

The effort to talk was noticeably difficult for Joe. He would often become winded and delay his words to breathe some oxygen to continue.

"Joe, that's a bad attitude. Do the doctors even know you're gay?"

"I'm sure they've figured it out. They got me in a room by myself, quarantined it seems. Anyone from the staff that comes in, comes in for just a second wearing protective gear that could protect them on the moon. In and out. They do what they have to do then get out. No one wants to linger."

"Have they said if you're getting better?"

Joe looked off to the side out a window that had only a view of a hazy blue sky. It looked like he was about to cry before he answered, "Gary, I don't want to be like this. I don't want to be sick."

Gary reached to gently take his friend's frail white hand. He consoled, "No one does, Joe, but you have to be patient until you get better."

"But I won't get better, you know that. I don't want to be in the hospital, and I don't want to be sick." Joe started coughing, the strain of exertion breaking a beady sweat across his forehead.

"Just relax," said Gary while moving Joe's pillow to make him a little more comfortable. He wiped off Joe's brow and almost wanted to cry when he made eye contact with his friend's fearful dark and suffering gaze. His hands became clammy, and the sweat from his friend seemed thicker and different from sweat he had felt before. Composing himself, he decided to be honest, and said, "It's hard for me to see you like this. It's scary."

"Believe me," Joe answered, "I wish I didn't have to put you through it. In some ways, except for the pain, I'm glad to have it happen. I don't have to worry anymore. Everything's out in the open, and now I just have to be done with it."

"You know. Many people live a long time after their first serious illness."

"They function. I wouldn't call that living."

"Are you afraid?"

"Quite frankly, Gary, ever since I was a kid I thought I wouldn't live to be thirty. Yeah, I guess I am afraid, even if I'm not all that surprised."

Gary held his friend tight. How foolish he had been to complain about the trials of his life. At first Joe almost recoiled because of the pressure, but then, he allowed himself to be hugged, because he was scared, and a buddy's comfort felt safe.

Finally, Joe thought, he touches me now that it's too late to matter. He whispered, "They all expect me to live. My father's always talking about when I get better. I think it's hardest on him. He's not one to show his feelings easily."

"You always thought he'd disown you if he found out you were gay. At least he's here."

"Yeah, still he upsets me. It's his duty to be here. If I wasn't sick, I wonder."

Gary couldn't understand why Joe still refused to accept his parents love at face value. There was no doubt his illness was grave, and a real possibility existed that it would kill him. His ego would then be destroyed for good, but instead of slowly fading away, it was making its last stand in a vain attempt to affirm itself at the very end.

Joe struggled to sit up and began to open a sugar packet to put in some ice tea he had to drink. He moved slowly, taking what to Gary seemed forever to just pick up the packet, and then an even longer time to barely be able to rip it open. Never in his life had Gary seen someone get so exhausted tearing only half of one of those little, tiny, flimsy, packets of sugar.

Still, he hesitated to help Joe, not wanting to make him feel helpless. But after he could stand it no longer, he patiently sweetened the tea for Joe and held the straw next his lips in order for him to drink. Joe looked relieved for the assistance, even though he never would have wanted to ask for it.

Gary said, "Are you tired of me yet?"

"It's hard for me to talk, but I'm glad you're here. Sit with me awhile…please."

So the two men sat in silence. Gary, now thirty, and suffering an emotional crisis because he believed his life had no meaning, and, Joe, a mere twenty-eight, finding his meaning to life through his death. More than a little shame filled Gary's heart for his pitiful self-indulgence.

Suddenly the silence was disturbed by an unannounced and never expected visitor. Jacole Smith-Rodriguez walked into the room.

Gary recognized Jacole, as did most any gay person living in San Diego longer than for a vacation, because of his, or as most people would say "her," "leadership" of the gay community. In the seventies, that leadership involved pimping prostitutes, male or female, to powerful people in need of such services, which is always an effective way of gaining political influence. Later, as the city grew and became more sophisticated, in an effort to legitimize himself, he instead turned back to leading his own community and became the proud sponsor of various sexploitation events that made him quite the person to impress if you happened to be young, gay, and in desperate need of self-respect. And much later, when the free sex he promoted led cruelly even if unknowingly to the plague, Jacole switched to social work, organizing the respected A.I.D.S.. Assistance Project. A dinosaur, Jacole was the standard bearer of an age that had managed to come out of the closet but could never change its wardrobe. He was a reactor, and an opportunist, however subconsciously, with little vision of how gay people might act positively in a world of acceptance.

Straight people, however, respected him for his work and looked to him as a spokesperson for his diverse community, even if Gary was more than a little resentful that this "Queen of Decadence" should all of a sudden turn over a new leaf in order to help those who suffered as a direct result of "her" past treatment of the body as an object of pleasure, and not something to be loved.

At his most cynical, Gary even believed Jacole's change of heart was contrived. After all, he did spearhead and glorify the environment that gave a fertile breeding ground to the virus, now he moved in to help those who fell its victim. Did he have a genuine change of heart? Did he feel guilt? Or, did he believe that a lending hand was just a more timely way to get the attention and power he had always lived for?

"Mr. Joseph Belisario? I am Jacole." Her Highness was grand.

Joe also knew of Jacole, but wondered why he had come to visit him in the hospital. At least he was wearing men's clothing, a business suit at that, even if he did sport a wide brim hat which looked a little flamboyant for Joe's more conservative taste in apparel.

"How do you know me, and that I was here?" he asked, still more curious than annoyed.

"Why child, the Project has people in every hospital. As soon as someone is admitted with an A.I.D.S. related illness a volunteer quickly contacts them to offer our support. I happened to be visiting some other people here, and I thought I would stop by on my way out to introduce myself and the Project to you."

Gary sat in stunned silence. Jacole was so bubbly, obviously very well pleased with himself because of all his good work. As the conscientious visitor reached into his briefcase, perhaps more appropriately described a purse, to get a brochure to leave with Joe, Gary watched the short, round, man, now moving on in years, do a good job of acting professional.

The last time Gary had seen Jacole was six years earlier at one of the infamous Jackie Awards balls. Then, he was in full women's drag, crowned with a tasteful tiara giving him the illusion of height he so badly needed to stand proud over his short stature. Despite the fact Gary had not actually seen him in public since, hardly a week went by that one of the local gay rags, euphemistically called "newspapers," didn't have an article singing the praises of San Diego's most notorious gay citizen.

Of course, the paper with the most praise was usually the one Jacole happened to own or be working for at the time. Most other forums attacked the selfish queen as someone most unworthy to represent a community as large as all men and women attracted to the same sex. Gary had always sided with the later feeling that Jacole would rather separate homosexuals from society rather than share with society another variety of experience.

Before him now stood the antithesis of his existence, an opportunistic, selfish, flamboyant, queen of the worst kind, willing to sell unsuspecting youths into pornography and then, when they became infected with disease, because they had been told that safe sex was not the thing people bought pictures of sex to see, took them in and supported them with a Project that was supposed to make the last days of their lives a little kinder and gentler. This was a person Gary could hate, and yet this was a person like himself doing the best he knew how no matter how misguided.

Jacole handed Joe the brochure and then looked straight at Gary. Never did he fail to make a stupid comment to a good-looking man. He said, "And who do we have here? Surely, you're someone I should already know."

Annoyed but still polite, Gary answered, "Why I'm Gary Nolan. And I've heard it's best to stay out of your way. I hear you can make or break anyone you wish, and I'd rather not take any chances."

"Vicious queens, all of them, that would say such a thing about little ol' me. Some people just can't stand anyone happier than themselves. I've never hurt anyone, that didn't deserve it that is, and Gary…" He reached over to tug at Gary's cheek. "…Gary, I can't imagine what could ever be wrong with someone as good looking as you. I am most pleased to meet you."

With a dramatically formal tone of feigned respect, Gary responded, "Likewise, I'm sure."

Then Jacole pulled himself together. "I must be off," he said with an animated swing of his hand and flippant toss of his head. "I've an important board meeting tonight at the Project. We're having trouble staffing our volunteer section and need to develop a new recruiting strategy. Gary, if you, or anyone else you know, can help, remember, it's our duty to help our brothers, like Joey here, in need." He pinched Joe on the cheek while checking his own appearance in the mirror on the far side of the bed before moving nearer the door to exit. "Toot-a-loo you two."

He was gone.

"Disgusting display," said Joe, obviously hurting to laugh. "And just when I was starting to feel a little better."

"Unbelievable," echoed Gary in agreement.

The visit continued for about another half hour. The two men hardly spoke as Gary helped Joe laboriously eat a piece of cheesecake that the doctors hoped would fatten him up. When Joe's mother returned to the room, Gary took his leave, saying he would return the next day for a visit. Joe said he was sure he wasn't going anywhere.

Riding down the elevator Gary felt drained of all emotion. A young doctor rode down with him reading the latest issue of *Money* Magazine. A hospital is a strange place, it is the beginning and ending of life, and yet it is first and foremost a business. Gary felt that he should be more upset by Joe's misfortune, but instead, he took the experience in stride. Joe, sadly, was the one sick. His role this time was to visit and offer support.

I'm no better than Jacole, he thought. Then, his mind turned to Josh and a memory of the weekend.

Confusion from his heart rushed up into his head. He had just seen a friend near death, a death precipitated by nothing more than the attempt to be loved. It was loving that was the cause of the dreaded plague. The Righteous called it God's curse on the homosexual not loving correctly. And it was hard to deny that the disease did seem to strike with a vengeance. But then how else would tragedy strike?

Joe had done nothing wrong to deserve his plight, except perhaps to look for love in a way he had been created to need. There is no choice in fulfilling one's nature, only the choice to deny that nature exists. If Joe had a choice, he surely would have chosen to get married and raise a perfect family in paradise. But paradise is a fantasy, and he found himself alive on Earth where, the Bible told him, the Creator made him in His image. What image is that then? The image of paradise, or the image of the world as it is found? For Joe, there was little time to decide.

His life was about to end. If he was to know love, he had better have found it already. But most likely, thought Gary, he had not, and was about to die anyway. Gary, on the other hand, may have found someone to love in Josh, but it was too soon to know that for sure. How easy it is to be in love after one weekend, how hard to feel the same after even a few days.

With the passing of time the daily routine of life moves in to surround a person, and with it the illusion of safety a routine brings. But safety can also breed boredom with its illusion everything remains the same. Eventually, one loses the sense of time in motion, and it seems there is all the time in the world to last forever. Until, one day when there is no time left to worry, because time has run out and you're about to die.

Arriving at home, Gary first checked his telephone answering machine. He was hoping to have a message from Josh. He wanted to get together with him, but figured that rightly Charlene should have first priority. Other times, he would have been jealous when he liked someone and knew they had other commitments. But it was hard to be jealous of his good friend Charlene. He already loved her, and was more than a little guilty for having become involved with her boyfriend in the first place.

But no message from Josh.

Gary opened himself a can of soup for dinner, turned on the television, and let the tube kill time for him until he finally dozed off to sleep. The Earth would turn bringing a different day, and with it perhaps a different attitude, and hopefully a more peaceful heart.

But his sleep was restless with fantasies of Josh, and when he woke up the first thing he wanted to do was call Josh before he went to work, but then he hesitated because Charlene may have spent the night with him, and it could be awkward having Gary call so early. Josh would then have to be short with him on the phone, and Gary would feel anxious all day long as a result.

No, it was better to wait for Josh to call him. If by chance he had changed his mind and no longer wanted to be friends, forcing him to talk would only make Gary look stupid for having a crush on someone now indifferent. Gary worked hard all day which kept his mind from thinking about it.

On his way home he stopped at the hospital to visit Joe. In the lobby sat an old black woman in a wheel chair waiting for a ride home. An oxygen tank was at her side and she could hardly breathe. Much like Joe, Gary thought. For a moment her eyes met his. There was a youthful quality to them, a longing, or maybe it was only an acknowledgment of Gary's strong, youthful, body.

Great, he thought, I can turn on an old lady.

Then, he recalled the woman of his vision when he was thrown off the bronco machine in San Felipe. The woman in his dream looked strikingly like the woman before him. Quickly he moved away from her when he thought he saw her smile knowingly at him.

Taking the elevator to the seventh floor, he walked to where he remembered Joe's room to be. Turning the corner into the doorway, he was startled to see an old man in Joe's bed. A younger woman leaned over him pulled up a blanket to make him more comfortable. She looked up at Gary, who said nothing but backed up and walked further down the hall.

When he was far enough away, he stopped and tried to remember exactly Joe's room number. Every corner of the hospital seemed to look the same, especially now that he was confused, but he was sure he had gone to the right place.

Next to the room he thought should be Joe's was another doorway with a screen pulled across it. By now Gary was more than a little upset. His heart beat rapidly and he felt sweat breaking on his palms. He thought about the real possibility that Joe had died, and that the hospital, efficient as it was, had already readied his room for a new patient.

Of course, Gary realized that there was always someone sick in need of care, but still he resented that there was no mention of the fate of the previous patient. What could they do? Post a sign that said, "To All Concerned: The Previous Patient is Dead." That would surely not be good for morale, or business.

Gary knew that Joe was not behind the screen, but his body moved toward it and pulled it away anyway in the vain and frantic hope that his friend was still alive. A nurse walked around the corner. Gary might have asked him about Joe, but was afraid of the answer, and too embarrassed that he, supposedly a good friend of the patient, was unaware of his fate.

The screen parted. Behind it the room was large and cold, with four single beds separated by a thin shower curtain hung like drapes. On each bed lay a man, or what looked to be a man, totally naked, completely covered with sores that oozed blood and puss. It was like their skin had fallen away to reveal an emaciated musculature clinging close to a skeleton already dead. But their eyes were wide open in pain. And each pair turned their attention toward him pleading to be released from their suffering.

Gary felt sick.

The men excited by his presence loudly moaned in agony. Gary believed he had walked into hell.

The nurse quickly entered the room. Mindful of Gary's potential state he said calmly, "Sir, I think you're in the wrong room." He grabbed Gary by the shoulders and helped him turn to walk back into the hall.

Gary was unable to speak. He was shaking from horror. Relieved to be away from the sight of such pain he asked, "What's wrong with them?"

"We don't know," said the nurse kindly. "Their bodies are rotting away but their spirits won't die. The room is supposed to be off limits to visitors. Not that anyone ever wants to come and see them."

"But what causes it?"

"A.I.D.S.."

Gary shuttered. Then he asked, "Do you know what happened to Joe Belisario who was on this floor yesterday."

"I'm sorry. I don't work on this floor. You'll have to ask the patient locator downstairs."

"Will they tell me if he's dead?"

"Are you family?"

"No."

"Well, I'm sorry they'll only tell the family. But if he's dead he won't be on the computer."

The nurse walked with Gary to the elevator. He was kind.

Half way down to the first floor a young couple got on board, obviously happy about seeing a newborn baby. When they realized Gary was upset, they became quiet. Their respect of his situation made him feel worse.

Everything about the first floor was business as usual. When Gary stood in line for the patient locator, he rehearsed in his mind how he would handle her telling him there was no record of Joe on the computer.

He practiced, "If there's no record of him does that mean he's dead?"

"Dead, or discharged," he imagined the receptionist to say without emotion.

In reality the exchange when differently. Gary asked for Joe Belisario.

As the receptionist typed in Joe's name, she recalled something and said, "Ah yes, I have a call out for a priest for him."

Gary was shocked that the woman could be so matter of fact. Did that mean he was dead, or dying?

She continued, "He's in intensive care. I guess he got worse over night."

Gary asked, "Can I see him?"

"Are you family?"

Gary accurately said, "No." Though he knew he was more likely family to Joe than his blood relatives.

"I'm sorry, then. Only family members are allowed to see him now. You need to contact them."

Gary said, "Thank you," and then walked away. He was frustrated because he did not know how to contact Joe's family. His friend was dying alone, and there was nothing he could do but go home and wait for someone to call him…and cry.

At home this time he had a message. He dreaded to hear bad news about Joe. But it was Josh asking he to go to dinner. Going to dinner was the furthest thing from his mind, and now Josh called. Life goes on, he thought. But still, Gary waited to call Josh back.

He wasn't ready to jump so hastily back into the water.

THREE WAY

Josh sat in his favorite chair trying to get interested in television. He sat alone, feeling especially empty while he waited for Gary to return his call. Already near eight, that afternoon he'd left a message on Gary's answering machine asking him out for dinner. Now, he wondered if Gary did not call because he was working late, annoyed with him, or else out with someone else. After all, the last time they parted they had not made any plans, and asking him to dinner was a last minute idea.

Josh knew analytical thinking of this kind was a waste of time. He knew Gary was the type of person to call as soon as he could. It was just that he really hoped to take Gary out that particular night, to talk to him, and be close to him again. Sex was not the reason, at least, he would not consciously admit to himself such a base motivation. What he wanted was to spend time with his friend and nothing more. Not being able to have this opportunity, Josh felt unsure about his new relationship.

He thought about driving over to Gary's house, in order to see if he was home, but avoiding him for some reason. He even got into his car and drove a few blocks down the road before realizing how silly he was acting. In the past, making a new friend would have been important enough to make himself a fool, but not now, now that maturity had started to temper his spunk into better sense.

For Gary's part, he had hoped for and heard Josh's message when he got home from the hospital around seven, and would have called him right back, but figured Josh would have already eaten something by then. Besides, he was not in the mood to be social, even with someone like Josh he wanted to know better. Instead, he heated some leftover spaghetti in the microwave, and ate it by candlelight in the breakfast nook of his dark kitchen.

The pasta which tasted good didn't settle well in Gary's stomach making him restless. Awake late into the night he read a boring book hoping to get drowsy. Usually, even a good book, would take less than a couple pages of reading to put him to sleep. But that night he was wound up. Frustrated, he put the book down and stared up at the ceiling. A cool breeze gently blew in through his window brushing across his oily face. He pushed off the top sheet with his leg to let the fresh air refresh his clammy nakedness.

"Release this day," he said out loud, remembering a meditation technique he had learned for relaxing. Instantly, and to his surprise, a weight was lifted from his soul. It was the power of his spoken word to remove the stress from his heart. Then he felt humble, for though hardly religious, Gary felt a power in his room that welcomed his trouble, a power that would gladly bear all the burdens he could load upon it, and Gary cried for being so arrogant to think he could deal with the hardships of his life alone. No one could, and it was relief to have a good cry over a world he could do nothing about.

He whispered rhetorically, "What the hell do we live for, if there is no escaping death?"

An image clearly formed in his mind of Joe sitting up in his mechanically-assisted hospital bed, his eyes begging for release. And Joe was not alone. All who suffer from disease make it impossible to ignore the inevitability of death, but all people, not just the sick, must die, and it seemed to Gary, who grew up in a time when death was discussed even less than sex, that to die was somehow to have failed. If that were true, then how could anyone hope to win?

In the afterworld, perhaps? But there was little room for a "sinner" like Gary in heaven. He wondered, was that his fear?—that death would be eternal damnation for a life lived poorly, and Joe's death of the dreaded disease God's way of making it perfectly clear that he, Gary Nolan, was also to suffer for his evil way of life supposedly chosen on Earth.

"Some loving God," he sobbed.

When life is good, it is easy to pretend that God is not important. But when all the horrible power of Nature rears up against itself it is not as easy to ignore the wrath of the Almighty. Even though Gary had read in the final chapters of *Job* that even this destructive power was a manifestation of Infinite love, he could not accept that what looked so horrible to human eyes could, in fact, really be love from any point of view.

It was hard to believe Joe was not cursed, and despite the philosophical claim that in experience there is no way to trace a cause from an effect, the power of science, and common sense for that matter, made it easy to believe that such a connection could be known, and in Joe's case was obvious. Joe had sinned, and now God punished him.

The advance of science has freed the human mind. But what of the human soul? Gary knew of no system of understanding with that kind of power. Etched in the primal memory was the warning: "To break a taboo is evil." And though much has been learned from self-reflection, few societies have learned to openly celebrate what is unique. The controlling power of culture is compelled to expound: "The evil shall suffer for their sins." And while our physical form may have evolved out of an ape, we still have not mutated beyond the crude morality of a monkey. No matter how enlightened we may feel, for humans, there must always be a threat to keep people in line.

Finally, the reflection ended and sleep came to Gary who escaped into a dream world. One dream in particular stood out. In it, Gary stood next to the crystal clear waters of a mountain lake. Small waves lapped gently against the pristine shoreline of course sand and polished stones. Up on a hill sat a woman in simple dress. She looked down on him from inside a stately grove of pines that whispered the wind's song of wisdom as it passed through them overhead. She wrote playfully in the dirt with her finger, and giggled to herself.

Gary walked slowly toward her, straining to see what she was spelling out. The woman, though, was indifferent until he got very close when she finally lifted her head. He was startled by what he saw. She was the woman of his visions, this time, however, younger and happier than when sitting alone in the green room, and healthier than when at the hospital. A warm smile greeted Gary. And it looked like she was trying to speak, but then the dream faded away, though not before Gary had a chance to see the word she wrote was "WELCOME."

The next morning, getting ready for work was hard for Gary. Before he left for the museum, he wanted to call the hospital to find out about Joe's condition. He picked up the phone but was afraid to dial the number. Joe was very sick, and Gary did not feel prepared to hear about the loss of his friend.

Entering the museum to do his janitorial work hours before the rest of the staff arrived, Gary's job was to clean the bathrooms and dust and mop the marble floors. Whenever it should happen that he was working late around other people, they would politely ignore him, like what he was doing was necessary, but beneath their higher stature of being concerned about the manifestations of talent hanging on the walls.

Many days, Gary would stand quietly alone, and gaze at the art, without the chatter of a pseudointellectual academic babble a crowd always brought with it. His favorite painting was Il Guercino's "The Return of the Prodigal Son." A little known example of Seventeenth Century art, it possessed, for him, the quality of something genuinely beautiful. It's color, subject, and proportion, mixed sublimely together to spark an emotion in his mind that was truly an aesthetic experience.

One time, while Gary was still working, two women from out of town were allowed into the Gallery before the public. They spoke softly as if in church, which Gary thought was odd, since no one else was around but him for them to disturb. They spent a lot of time discussing the Cezanne and Rembrandt. And of course, they loved the David and couldn't chitchat enough about Eastman Johnson's "Cranberry Harvest." But when they came to the Il Guercino, they just walked by making some mumble about "it being nice," not for a second allowing themselves the chance to experience the spiritual beauty Gary found in the painting by a man whose name was not widely known.

These women, like most everyone else who visited the museum, missed it completely, the beautiful scene of the old patriarch welcoming home his son stripped bare by the misfortune of his childish ignorance about his birthright, a heavenly estate of true spiritual prosperity. Humbled by the love of his father, the youth shed lovely tears of gratitude at being unconditionally accepted home.

That morning, when Gary looked at the painting he saw it as if for the first time. Could it be that there are other memories from the past hidden in our minds, memories of love and forgiveness from some time before we were born? Was this the truth that Christ illuminated with his parable, and Il Guercino captured with his masterful skill of the brush? Gary wondered if the only barrier to heaven was a man's fear to let himself return? And then he wondered, if he wasn't the son that stayed behind.

Finished mopping, he sat at a small wooden desk in the guards room and mustered the courage to dial the hospital's patient locator number on the old rotary style phone. His fingers ached from the laborious task by the time he was done.

"Good morning, Scripps Memorial," answered a friendly woman's voice.

"Yes," he choked. A dry throat made it hard for him to speak. Nervously, he continued, "Could you please tell me if you have a patient there by the name of Joe Belisario?"

"One moment, sir."

Gary could easily feel beating of his heart and the rush of blood to his head.

"Sir, I show no Joe Belisario admitted." She was courteous and cheerful.

Gary paused for a moment to remember his friend. Then he thanked the receptionist of the information, like he might have called the wrong hospital so she would not have to feel his pain, and then he hung up.

Only later did he resent that the she couldn't say, "I'm sorry, Hun…but someone you loved has just died."

The previous night had been restless for Josh also. He waited for Gary to call until it was very late, too late for them to get together. He waited even longer to at least plan to get together another night. Near midnight, he finally gave up hope and went to bed frustrated.

The next morning he resisted calling Gary first thing, aware enough to realize that his main reason for calling would be to check up on Gary to see if he spent the night at home. Not that the question hadn't crossed his mind as to whether Gary had another lover. His infatuation with Gary made him think it was better he didn't know the answer to that question just yet. If Gary didn't call by that evening, he would try him again later.

When Josh got home from work that afternoon there was a message on his machine. Not waiting to play it back, he knew it had to be from Gary. Optimism saved him suffering. Josh quickly picked up the phone to call his infatuation right back.

"Hello," answered the deep, sexy, voice of his friend.

"Yeah, Gary, this is Josh. You busy?" He played it cool.

"Nope," said Gary, thinking, Shit…and I never called him back. "Hey guy I'm sorry I didn't call you last night, but I'd sure like to get together for dinner some time."

"Don't worry about it," said Josh relieved it was irresponsibility and nothing more. "Have you eaten yet?"

"Not yet."

YES! thought Josh. "Then you wanna get something tonight. I can pick you up in twenty minutes."

Doesn't want to waist any time. Kinda nice, Gary thought, for a change. "Sounds great. See ya when you get here."

A matter of fact exchange true to the formula for making a date in California. Neither revealed the anguish and hope in their hearts, Gary's anguish over the loss of his friend, or Josh's hope about finally confronting his homosexuality.

On Gary's suggestion they ate downtown at a small Japanese-American bistro that catered to the up-and-coming college crowd, young professionals, and art fags dressed in black and speaking in well-honed accents of pretentious intelligence. The servings were generous at a reasonable price so the surcharge of phoniness was easy enough to take. The room was brightly lit and sparsely decorated, the colorfulness of the clientele providing more than enough atmosphere. The lovebirds sat at a small table in the back and split a large Japanese beer while they looked over the menu and made small talk to become better acquainted.

Josh poured the beer giving it a good head and took a big gulp. "I can't believe we've known each other for over a year and are just now getting better acquainted."

Gary smiled a little uncomfortably since Gary's remark indirectly but pointedly touched the tender nerve of his relationship with Charlene. He fumbled for words of response. "You always did seem nice, but you are dating Charlene. I would've never expected you thought about being Gay."

Josh didn't like the sound of that word. "I don't know if I'd call myself *that*."

Gary chuckled, "What would you call it then when you like to play with another man's genitals?"

Josh blushed concession behind his glass lifted for a drink.

Gary continued, "What does Charlene think about us getting along?"

"Don't know, for sure. I haven't known what to tell her."

Gary was insensitive to Josh's uneasiness. "She's a smart one. I'm sure she'll catch on, soon enough."

Gary loved Charlene, and would hate to do anything to hurt her, but she and Josh, like many straight couples, weren't all that close even though they dated regularly. Still, Charlene had often spoken kindly of Josh to Gary. She did like him, but always felt there was some barrier around him preventing her from expressing a real commitment of love. Josh acted like he loved her, sometimes so much so it was frightening. His actions were too contrived and perfect. Charlene couldn't pinpoint it, but she long ago confided with Gary that something was wrong. They were not compatible.

Gary, now more enlightened, figured Josh's "barrier" was really a desire to explore being with a man. For Gary, this desire was something that had always been conscious in him. The hard thing to accept was that this feeling was natural, not self-indulgent. After all, he also liked women and was even sexually attracted to them on occasion. Not in the way a "straight" man is supposed to be, but when a woman was his type, his penis got as hard as anyone's.

It made Gary feel that maybe the labels of hetero-or homo-sexual were misplaced, that maybe people were just sexual, to varying degrees and dispositions. He could have passion for a woman, but that passion was always tempered by respect for the values of society. To take advantage of a woman seemed wrong to Gary, but he thought nothing of seducing a man. He wondered if Josh might not be just the opposite case, not afraid to have his way with a woman, but more observant of American society's revulsion of two men having sex.

"What kind of music do you like?" asked Josh, changing the subject to something less threatening.

Gary hesitated to answer. Certainly Charlene had mentioned to Josh his eclectic taste in music, a taste he often hated himself for having developed. Josh probably expected Gary to say pop, rock, disco, or country, the four acceptable drags of modern society. But Gary liked all kinds of music, and felt comfortable with himself for his diversification even though it made others see him as odd.

"I like all kinds of music," said Gary, not yet ready to rise onto a soapbox about the merit of his taste.

"Me too," said Josh, who had not been exposed to even a fraction of the music Gary about, but was honest in saying that he was open to the different styles he had heard.

Gary tested Josh's sophistication by asking him if he ever heard of the African superstar Salif Keita.

"Never heard of him," was his response.

And Gary's omen for equality with his new friend looked bad. He decided to change the subject and let Josh off the hook, "Maybe sometime you're over at my place we can listen to him."

Rashly seizing the opportunity to be alone with Gary at his place, Josh blurted, "How 'bout tonight."

An advance which took Gary off guard. Now, when he thought back to how he felt only a few days before driving home from Mexico, he knew he also had interest in being with Josh. But the unexpected death of Joe had shaken some of the lust out of his spirit, and replaced it with the less impulsive realization that what he was doing was stealing his best friend's lover.

Hesitantly Gary replied, "I suppose that would be fun."

"Don't sound so excited," quipped Josh, acutely aware of Gary's uneasiness.

"It's not that," said Gary. "I was thinking of Charlene." He decided to use the easiest reason for his hesitation.

"We're just going to listen to some music," returned Josh, naively oblivious he intended to do much more.

"Right," agreed Gary, unable to resist the seduction of a man he found so attractive, at a time when he really needed someone to hug.

At home, Gary put on the African music and Josh was enthralled with its exotic beat. The sound had a contemporary jazz-like quality, and if you ignored that much of the singing was in a foreign language, it sounded just about like any other well-produced record of the day. Gary kept the volume low so that it would not grow tiresome.

After getting them each a beer Gary lied down on his couch. Josh sat in a chair across from him. A marine layer from the ocean cooled the evening off. Still, Gary left the front door open to allow the fresh air to blow through the room. With a remote control he turned on one small light that cast large shadows up the walls and cove ceiling like the flicker of a candle.

"Like the music?" he asked Josh.

"Sounds great. It's not weird at all."

Well, that was a good sign for Gary. He had chosen the album because it was accessible, but that had not stopped other people from commenting on its strangeness.

Then, Josh surprised Gary by seriously asking with concern, "Gary, you seem distant. Is something wrong?"

Touched by the selflessness of his friend to recognize that he was suffering, he answered honestly, "I didn't want to say anything to ruin the evening, but a good buddy of mine got sick while we were in Mexico. He died this morning."

Josh instantly got up from his chair and walked over to the couch to comfort Gary who was obviously upset. "I'm sorry to hear that. Were you two close?" Josh squeezed behind Gary to give him a solid hug.

"We never dated, or anything. But sometimes that can let you care more about someone."

"Was he sick for long?"

"A couple of weeks is all, but he said it was just the flu. I talked to him just last Wednesday and he said he was feeling better, but over the weekend I guess the pneumonia got so bad it killed him."

"You don't hear of too many young people dying of pneumonia nowadays."

"Well, he didn't have regular pneumonia. He had a complication related to A.I.D.S.."

"Oh."

There was an awkward silence between the two men. Gary knew that it probably was a bad time to bring up A.I.D.S., but it was on his mind, and it was something that two men thinking about having sex shouldn't ignore.

Josh finally said, "I don't like to think about that."

"I'm sorry I brought it up."

"Don't be sorry. It's not your fault your friend got sick and died. It scares me, that's all."

"Yeah, me too."

Josh's hand slowly caressed Gary's stomach, and he lightly kissed his friend on the back of the neck. Gary closed his eyes and allowed the pleasurable sensation to push the feelings of fear and loss from his mind and heart.

Gary said, "I'm glad you called."

"That's good, because I was afraid I was bugging you."

"I was at the hospital until late last night. Otherwise, I would have called you right back."

"You never can tell why people do what they do. I thought you might have been spooked because of Charlene."

"Well, that does bother me a little."

"We've never talked about committing ourselves to seeing each other exclusively."

"Does she know you date men?"

"No. Besides, you're the first man I've ever been with intimately."

Gary thought that must be a lie because Josh seemed too smooth, but decided not to start a confrontation. Maybe it was true. He hoped to trust Josh.

Taking note of Gary's lack of response, Josh emphasized foolishly, "It's true."

"I'm flattered," said Gary with a teasing tone in his voice.

"Go ahead. Don't believe me, if you want."

"Believe you me," said Gary seductively. "That is not what I want."

And then, as if to show Josh what it was he did desire, Gary turned around and planted a kiss right on Josh's sexy lips, his tongue probing into the mouth of his friend in a most passionate embrace. The two men stopped talking and began exploring each other's body as they slowly discarded every stitch of their clothing.

When they both lay naked, Gary suggested that they move into the bedroom, taking their play to a more serious arena.

Silent now, and to the glow of a real candle that burned on Gary's night stand, the boys explored each others masculinity. It was somewhat more awkward than it had been in San Felipe. There, the spontaneity of Josh's advance had made it easy for the encounter to be charged with excitement. Now, both men were self-conscious about their movements, and as a result their advances were much more contrived.

Most disturbing to Gary was Josh's natural pattern of having sex with Charlene. Josh was unaware that he possessed a routine, but Gary, who had been with enough men to recognize that people do fall into ruts when it comes to sex, picked up on Josh's groove almost immediately. Josh was the "straight" man taking charge of his woman. Of course, he realized that Gary was a man, and so he did not fall exactly into character, but Gary still felt uneasiness in his friend when he switched roles and forcibly flipped him onto his stomach and began licking the small of his back and fondling his firm buttocks.

Normally, with someone Gary was not that interested in knowing for long, he would have enjoyed playing with a mind that had not yet evolved enough to laugh at itself. It had taken him many years to outgrow a pathological preoccupation with sex that American culture instilled in him without providing any way for him to be relieved since his drive was not normal. The contradictory mix of signals, on the one hand telling him to have sex, on the other, not to copulate, created a bad psychological atmosphere in which to grow up. Gary was not alone, hardly anyone he knew had good sex.

Josh, becoming aware that sex with Gary was indeed something different from with Charlene, or the other women he had been with (since he always treated every woman pretty much the same), he decided to take advantage of the situation and let himself go in order to have fun in ways he had always suppressed. He started to wrestle with Gary, and the two men tossed and turned, at first playfully, but later as the sexual tension grew with greater urgency. Josh found the strong resistance of his muscular companion a turn on, especially since his greater agility allowed him to remain somewhat in control.

Flipping Gary over onto his stomach, Josh admired the strong back, buttocks, and legs of his new buddy. With one hand he pressed Gary's shoulder to the bed, with the other he lifted his stomach, feeling the furrows of its musculature, so that his partner was up on all fours. Mocking the motion of butt fucking his friend, Josh found the action made him rock hard.

Gary did not particularly like being dominated by another man, even though it was the masculinity of a date that attracted him at first. Every man is different in the degree that masculinity and femininity are expressed in their behavior. For that matter, every person, male or female, alive in this world is the same way. Even though it may be convenient for small minds to stereotype behavior in order to organize the world in such a way to make sense of it, in reality there are very few rules of nature for which there are no exceptions.

Sometimes Gary would enjoy dominating, sometimes he would enjoy being submissive. He didn't like to play the same role every time. Many people he knew had become comfortable in playing one role. It was easier for them to repress parts of themselves than to come to grips with the full spectrum of feelings a human body is able to manifest. Even Gary knew it would be easier to just give in and play a role. It was a lot easier to find a compatible date that way. Trying to find someone who was secure enough with their own sexuality to be completely spontaneous had resulted in Gary spending many nights alone with his hand as his only companion.

As he knelt there on all fours, it occurred to Gary that he found the situation rather stimulating, though at the same time a little disturbing. Did Josh think that Gary was just a substitute for the women he had known? It bothered Gary that Josh had maneuvered himself into the dominant role. Most men would try to do this, at least initially. It was part of the garbage of our culture that if a man allows himself to be dominated he is worthless. Of course, the same should be said for women, who have really no choice but to be dominated in that way. It may be true there are dominant women, but the bottom line in Gary's experience was that true dominance was determined by penetration. While a woman might strap on a dildo and plow her boyfriend, she could only do so with the aid of a device that made it perfectly clear she lacked the necessary equipment needed to be naturally "superior".

Gary thought all of this garbage was bullshit, but since he was just one man in a society that, even in denial, still succumbed to the timeless rules of the past, he could still not help feeling a bit funny when Josh made his move to penetrate him.

"Woe!" said Gary.

Josh pulled back. He said, "What's wrong?"

"Don't you think you forgot something?" he asked. Gary had decided to allow Josh to enter him, but not without the protection of a condom the times demanded. Of course, his having to tell Josh to put on a rubber was very awkward, and instantly killed the spontaneity and magic of the moment.

For Josh's part, he had never thought of using a rubber. The women he had known always used the pill to prevent pregnancy, and he never thought about getting a social disease. He asked naively, "What?"

"A rubber. I have one in the top drawer there."

Josh, still thinking that a person only used a condom to stop pregnancy, was confused that Gary would want him to put one on. He thought, certainly Gary wasn't worried about getting pregnant. He asked, "Why?"

"Don't you know the best way to spread A.I.D.S. is by getting fucked?" Gary was more than a little irritated by having to bring up the subject of A.I.D.S. while he was making love. It was like having a three way with a person you despised. Fun sex was as good as over.

Josh lost his hard on, and sat against the headboard of Gary's bed. Gary sat next to him.

Josh said, "But I don't have A.I.D.S. Do you?"

"I was tested once, and was negative. I'd like to keep it that way."

"But there is no time I could have ever been exposed," said Josh.

"You don't know that for sure," said Gary. "Maybe you just don't remember, and who knows when it might have happened. I think it's better if we're careful."

"I feel like you think I'm diseased."

"No. It might be me that could infect you."

"But I'm not worried about that," said Josh. "I want to be with you. And I like you. There's nothing dirty about what we're doing. When two people care about each other, how could that be the breeding ground for disease?"

Gary felt bad for even bringing up the subject. Maybe, he thought. He was being paranoid. After all, he believed Josh had only been with women, and the likelihood of him being exposed to the virus was minimal. Since Gary had never been sick, and he had tested negative, it seemed that Josh was right that they should not be at too great a risk.

Then, Gary remembered Joe, and horrible way the disease had taken his friend, who as far as he knew was a good person. The image should have scared him into greater care, but somehow the idea that the plague could be so indiscriminate frightened Gary in such a way that it was easier for him to rationalize away the threat and deny its reality than to accept the responsibility to protect himself. Instead of fearing a sexual encounter, he longed for an encounter that was better than ever. Josh seemed ideal.

Josh moved to give Gary a strong, sensual, kiss, and the two men slowly began to embrace. After a few minutes, both of their pasts were forgotten in the immediacy of the magic moment. They abandoned all inhibition, and properly consummated their relationship in complete repression of the danger with which they were flirting.

TRUE LOVE

Charlene slammed the door to her office, flopped frustrated into her chair, and laid her head down on the cluttered desktop. She was angry enough to kill. Her editor just cut a story she worked on for months, for no other reason, he said, than that it was suddenly "inappropriate" for the kind of paper he hoped to circulate.

A lame excuse, thought Charlene, well aware of the story's controversial nature, especially for the fluff-filled Society section of the paper. Why else would she have taken so much care to explain it in detail to him and get his approval even before starting the research. He showed excitement about it then.

Most likely the publisher got wind that the story dealt with one of her personal friends. Later, a sweet phone call to the editor, and no censorship exercised, the story regardless of its newsworthiness, or truth, became inappropriate for the kind of paper being published.

Charlene did not doubt that Dora Divine-Snorton deciding to give the Timken Art Museum a graciously generous grant of one million dollars should be considered news. After announcing her intentions Dora instantly became the Grande Dame of San Diego Society. A paradox of sorts, considering the more than humble birth of Dora as Lucy Lang of the Lang Egg Ranch outside of Ramona in North County, and one Charlene felt was worthy of a story.

Charlene's first meeting with Dora revealed a contradiction in the aristocratic lady's air of grandeur and phoney accent of sophistication. Not so far beneath the skin, Dora remained a down-home girl all fancy spangled with cut glass and cheap perfume. Only luck let her meet and fall in love with Jimbo Snorton before he made millions selling the ubiquitous "Snorton Chew," a tobacco-less concoction that younger men and women believed made them look cool. Everywhere, it became the fad rage to chew, and a mother's only objection to the habit, since the juice was supposed to contain vitamins and minerals for one's health, was that the kids tended to spit the gooey brown sludge it produced without concern to where it might fall.

Dora, garishly, from a lack of good breeding, had admitted to the director of the Timken that the idea for the gift was advised by her husband's accountant, who wanted to offset some of the tax liability the couple had incurred with the Chew's remarkable success. Gary, the janitor, and close friend of Charlene (a connection no one in the gallery suspected was possible), had overheard this one day. And, of course, he couldn't wait to tell his contact at the paper about it.

The best part of the story, however, was that Dora had attached an outrageous condition to her philanthropy. She wanted the Museum to construct a fountain in the foyer in her name, so that the first nameplate anyone read upon entering the museum would be one that paid homage to the living Grand Dora Divine-Snorton's good will, and not some "dead artist without influence," as she so simply put it.

Gary found the whole situation hysterical, because Dora and her money had the Museum by the balls, and her supposed generous support of the arts, if accepted, while giving her a big name in the art world, would actually do more damage to the works of art on display than if she had just stuck her finger of fortune right through them.

A principal concern of any museum is the preservation of the works of art in its possession. A great deal of money consequently is spent each year maintaining a suitable environment inside the Museum to minimize the damage that exposure to the environment can have on the fragile treasures displayed. Controlling the humidity in the space was of great concern for maintaining the paintings. The presence of a fountain would make it all the more difficult, especially with the antiquated air-conditioning equipment in the building.

Dora, though, would hear none of this chatter about what was good for the art. Either the museum wanted the money, or it did not. The world was simple for her. It was only after long deliberation and much perturbation that the Board of the Timken finally rejected her proposal like someone about to dive into an ice cold lake in the mountains. They estimated that the damage done to the art by the fountain would, in short time, cost far more to repair than the million generous dollars the Divine-Snorton was willing to donate.

Unforseen by the Board, however, their decision was a double-edged sword. Not only did they cut themselves by not acquiescing to the condition of the grant, they also inadvertently near-mortally cut Dora by humiliating her before her caddish peers.

It was rare that a large sum of money was ever given without some spoken or unspoken strings of attachment. But it was always important to the benefactor most interested in looking generous, that a gift appear to all the world as unconditional. When the rest of high society found out that Dora was so shockingly self-centered as to demand a fountain in her own name, and as gossip enhanced the story, they self-righteously reduced the dame from the toast of the town into a laughing stock overnight. Charlene found all this amusing and a good story because despite all the brew-ha-ha, Dora's indiscretion was really harmless, since it was attached only to false pride, and not greed, which most of the others had been guilty at one time or another.

Charlene's article documented the rise and fall of San Diego's former Queen of Culture. She thought it turned out rather well. Funny and sad, it was politically correct to illustrate how dangerous it is to give, supposedly out of kindness, but with the ulterior motive of getting something in return for oneself.

"Unfortunately," her editor said coolly, "that kind of in-depth journalism does not sell papers."

But Charlene knew better, that kind of dirt about the famous is exactly what sells papers. The problem with her story was that her dirt happened to be on a good friend of the publisher. So much, she thought, for a free press in America.

The phone rang. It was Gary on the line asking her to meet him for lunch.

"Sure," said Charlene.

Gary, sensing an irritation in her voice, and guiltily thinking it had to do with him asked, "You upset?"

"This fucking paper! They rejected my story on Snorton."

"Awe!," exclaimed Gary, genuinely sympathetic with Charlene's irritation, but glad she was not angry with him. There was no reason that she should know about him and Josh, but still he was paranoid that she would find out before he had a chance to tell her himself. He added, "I thought you had your editor's okay on that before you even started working on it."

"Yeah, I did. But that bitch publisher turns out to know Snorton, who has a bug in her ear. Dora probably called her up and cried that any more publicity, especially anything having to do with the truth, would ruin her." Charlene couldn't help herself from laughing, "That's a riot. She's the one who jumped into the casket. I was just lowering her into the ground."

"Well, except for the time you spent working on it, maybe it's just as well to let it be over with for everyone's sake."

"I understand that," said Charlene curtly. "But that's exactly the problem with journalism today. We jump on the breaking story, but never get to follow up on anything. God forbid we ever try to make sense of anything, or put it in perspective."

"Don't get started, Charlene. This is your buddy Gary. Remember, I've heard all this before."

"I know." She took a deep breath. "I'm sorry. Where do you want to meet for lunch?"

"Why don't you get a sandwich, and meet me in the park at our usual spot."

"Sounds good, Gar."

"Good," said Gary. "See ya then."

Charlene put down the phone. That's odd, she thought. It had been quite awhile since Gary had asked her out for lunch. She wondered what he wanted to see her about.

Gary bought his sandwich and walked to the bottom of the grassy hill where he was to meet Charlene. The park was crowded that afternoon with tourists visiting "America's Finest City." A young couple roller skated past him as he sat down on the towel he laid out on the grass. The girl was perpetually falling, laughing all the way. Her youthful date was trying to act in control, though he too looked about as steady as a bowl of Jell-O on the move.

Across the lawn, near the edge of the canyon, sat a motley crew of park bums, their packs and shopping carts arranged in a circle. Their clothes were torn and dirty, yet still artfully worn with some kind of fashion. One man seemed to be telling the others a story which everyone listened to carefully and seemed to enjoy. A young woman wearing tight shorts, a stretch top, and headphones danced ceaselessly behind him. They all looked very content, which gave Gary pause to think.

Cars drove quickly down the side road through the park. Men and women in business suits met to take a break from working downtown. Some sat kissing in the car, others went for strolls on the paths that led through the tall groves of eucalyptus and pine.

Gary lay on his stomach looking up the hill. A young man was walking away from him up it. His hair was unkept and he had a few weeks worth of scraggly beard. He walked behind his wheelchair, walked with his legs twisted and his feet turned inward. He walked up the hill by himself with what looked like a great deal of effort. His life's work was walking.

The whirl of activity around the young man made him look like the eye of a hurricane. But right around him calm radiated from his soul. He looked like an angel to Gary, his sole purpose to get up the hill. He had no concerns for employment, or the chance for love. His deformity took care of these worries of busy men.

Gary wondered if the man was ever sexually aroused. Of course, he thought, feeling stupid. But what could he do? Suddenly, Gary felt an attraction for him. He was attracted to the immediacy of his action, to a world without understanding, a world lived unconsciously like an animal.

"Friend," a soothing voice said from behind him.

Gary turned, to see a beautiful black woman standing behind him. Her dark skin glistened in the sunlight. Her strong features were clearly of darkest African descent. Something about her caused time to slow down, to make the moment linger.

She said, "Are you waiting for someone?"

Gary sat stunned. The woman seemed so familiar, but he could not remember meeting anyone like her before. Then, it came to him that this woman was the same old woman of his visions. But now she was beautiful and young. She wore the clothes of a bum, but somehow irradiated them with a spectacular light of love. The colors were bright in the sun. Her smile was big, and melted his busy and confused heart.

"Yes," Gary managed to squeak out of a dry throat.

She asked predictably without a hint of awareness of what he perceived her to be, "Can you spare any change, man?"

Gary reached into his wallet to give her a dollar. As he handed it to her, he heard Charlene shout from out of her car atop the hill. He turned to look at her.

"Gary! Sorry I'm running a little late. I've got to get my sandwich still. I'll be right back."

"Okay," he called back.

She then sped off down the road. And when Gary turned back around to ask the Black woman where she was from, she was gone. He turned again to see the Cripple, but he too had vanished. Gary wondered if he was losing his mind, but instead of worrying about it, decided to lie back in the sun and take a short nap while he waited for Charlene to return. He was going to tell her about his affair with Josh, and he figured his fear of her reaction was putting him under too much stress.

Gary's eyes closed, removing him from the world for a moment, though, the bright disc of the sun still made its mark in his mind as a great red spot of veiled brightness. One spot at first, then two overlapping, then, many more, that danced in circles across his field of view. A cluster of brilliant white lights dancing from the right side of the world into the red. The meeting caused sprays of violet, orange, and blue color to wash together in an impressionistic spectacle that touched the soul, but left the mind in wonder.

Then, Gary found himself floating face up in a pond of still blue water. The water was warm and soothing, and though he was not touching the bottom, he made no effort to stay afloat. On the shore he saw a small group of women doing their wash. They laughed and told stories to the rhythmic beat of the laundry hitting the large cleaning stones. The steady pounding, and the incomprehensible drone of their conversation, hypno-tized him.

Suddenly, he found himself on land inside of a shack that was in com-plete order, if poorly constructed. Gary moved into its back room. A young child lay there, on a small bundle of rags in a dark corner. Gary moved closer to the child, who upon inspection looked to be very sick. Taking the boy into his arms, Gary felt helpless. He knew of no way to bring the fragile life back to good health. Moving to kiss the child, he was startled to see a smile on its small face. Surely, he thought, someone so sick must be suffering.

But with the smile, poured a heavenly light through the child's eyes, a light that encircled Gary's body and made him quite hot, so hot in fact, that he began to worry he would catch fire. Putting the boy down, he turned and ran out of the house to find some way to cool himself off.

Outside, he saw a small stream running across a meadow close by. He ran into the cool water, splashing it onto his sizzling skin, drinking it to quench his parched throat. Back inside the house he heard the shrieks of a woman. She wailed something about her child being murdered. A town-full of people amazingly sprung up around Gary, who did not notice them coming while he was drinking his relief.

"Why have you killed the child?" asked the booming voice of one of the men.

Gary answered timidly, "But I did not kill anyone. The boy was sick. There was nothing I could do to save him."

The hysterical mother then moved up to Gary. In her arms she held a bloody bundle that could be none other than the boy. Gary was shocked. How could his putting the child down have done so much harm?

The woman stood facing Gary. She spoke, now in a calm voice, though one still trembling with emotion, "What will you do now, that you have destroyed our only hope for happiness?"

"How could that sick child," he asked, "have brought you any joy?"

"But he was not sick!" the woman snapped back.

"But I saw it with my own eyes. The boy was near death."

"Near death, perhaps," said the woman. "But still he gave me so much love, so much joy." The woman sobbed.

Gary stood confused. The townspeople were not angry with him. Several even came over to give him a hug.

A young girl came and took his hand. She led him away from the crowd who continued to console the woman. She led him down to a clearing between a grove of tall pines. There, she took up a handful of dirt and place a small amount of it in her mouth, eating it with gusto. She then gave some to Gary. Tasting it, to his surprise it was edible, and tasted quite good.

"You're new here," said the girl.

"No," said Gay, a little surprised by his own word.

"Then you are newly born, despite your appearance of age. It matters little to anyone here. You have touched the child. It is an omen."

"An omen?"

The girl smiled, and as Gary was just beginning to take notice of her beauty, and her image, she dissolved into a stream where Gary saw her become a blurred reflection of himself. He was in the high mountains now, far above the tree line, and close, so close to the stars of heaven. He had grey hair and a beard, and looked very, very, old.

A cold wind blowing down from a spectacular cirque sent a chill to his bones as he walked back to his small hut beneath the billion twinkling stars of an unpolluted night sky. He stood beneath the Milky Way and recognized each light above as the campfire of someone he knew.

"Hey, Gary!…Wake up!"

Charlene had returned with her food.

"I must'a fallen asleep."

She said, "It must be nice, being under so much pressure. I'm so pissed at Ericson."

"But what can you do?"

"I can't believe she had the balls to cut my story."

"And when you said she had already approved the idea."

"She did! Until, it happened that Dora was best friends with you know who, and it came down from on high that it wasn't news the paper was interested in publishing."

"I'm sorry, Charlene. You spent a lot of time working on that story."

"Well, at least Ericson will give me credit for that."

"I heard something at the Museum today that might cheer you up."

Charlene's interest instantly became perked. She had journalism in her blood.

Gary continued, "It seems the Mayor is causing a stink about the opening reception of the Art Festival."

"I thought you guys were putting that on as a benefit for him?"

"Well, there were to be two parties, one for the Museum's Friends, and one for the Mayor's entourage. The Timken was going to pay for both of them, but when the Mayor found out that his party was the night after our Friend's, he was very disturbed."

"What difference would it make? There'd be no press at the Friends function?"

"I guess it made a difference to him. Because he forced the Director to cancel both parties, which would be a relief for everyone, except that our friend Snorton was to give some kind of commemoration to the Mayor at the affair, which was to be a kind of appeasement since the Boards decision. She called this morning, and was having a cow."

"Unbelievable." Charlene shook her head. "But I doubt the way the paper is acting about Snorton that there's any news in that for me."

"I just thought you get a kick out of it."

"Is that what you wanted to tell me about?"

"Actually," Gary paused. "No." He took a bite out of his sandwich. "I wanted to talk to you about something else."

"What, then?" asked Charlene, curious to have the mystery solved. Gary was obviously at a loss for words.

"Well, I don't know exactly how to begin."

"Oh, Gary. Are you in some kind of trouble?"

"Some kind of trouble, yes." He asked, "How are you and Josh getting along these days?"

"You know something about Josh?"

Gary did not reply, but her looked confirmed that she was beginning to understand.

She played along, and answered her friend. "I don't know. I really haven't talked to him much lately. Even before we went to San Felipe things weren't going too well, but since then he's been more distant than ever."

"What do you think the problem is?"

"I don't know what it is for him, but for me it has to do with sex."

"How do you mean?"

"He's not interested in me anymore. I don't know what's wrong. I don't want to sound vain, but I think I'm a good-looking woman. And he says he's attracted to me. That's not the problem. But there's always some preoccupation with him. It could be that I'm just paranoid, cleverly he sets it up that way, but my intuition tells me something's wrong."

"Well, I think you're right."

"What do you know?"

"He made a pass at me in San Felipe."

"Really?" She thought it over. "That would explain a lot. Except that he knows I know, and like, you, and that I know you're gay. Why didn't he just tell me when we met that he inclined toward being gay?"

"Maybe, he doesn't really know himself. He talks like he's just coming out."

"You've talked to him then, since the trip?"

It bothered Gary that Charlene was acting so cool. When she first met Josh, she had told him often how this guy was the most special man she had met in some time. And Charlene was not a woman to fall in love easily. Most of the time people thought she used her job to sublimate any interest in romance. She was good at her work, but it was only because she enjoyed it. Gary knew this, but he also knew that Charlene was not completely fulfilled in her job. She did not use it as a substitute for love, and would not settle for less than was good for her. When she met Josh, she had thought she had found a man she could spend her life with.

"Yes, I've talked with him since the trip." Gary felt good to have his betrayal out in the open with his best friend. His sense of relief spurred him to talk frankly, no longer sidetracking the issue to protect her feelings. "He says he's in love with me."

"Oh, he does, does he. Kind of fast to fall in love, don't you think?"

"Please don't be angry with me."

"I'm only upset with myself for being such a fool."

"You're not a fool to care for someone."

"I am a fool! Because I saw this coming, not with you of course, but I could tell Josh was having those kinds of feelings, but I denied it because I am selfish. Now, I'm paying the price."

"Charlene, you are a beautiful woman." Gary gently wiped the tear falling down her cheek as he spoke.

"Beautiful, some joke. What has beauty ever got me?"

"I wasn't talking about how you looked."

Charlene smiled. "You dog! Steal my man, and flatter me too."

They both started laughing. They had a great deal of history between them.

Gary said, "I didn't tell you this to hurt you, or to get Josh in trouble. I don't know what he'd think about us talking. But we've been friends for too long for me to keep it a secret from you. I like him. And if he wants to be with a man, I'd like to be able to do it with him."

"Why, Gary…are you asking my permission?"

"Not your permission, but your understanding."

"What can I say?"

"You don't have to say anything right now. I'm sure it will take awhile for you to know how you feel."

Charlene wiped her eyes with her napkin, then took a bite out of her sandwich. She chewed it in silence that Gary respected. Then, exhaling audibly, she remarked, "What a day! You wake up thinking you're in a rut, and then the world makes it perfectly clear how stupid you can be not to realize that lightening can strike at any time."

"Charlene…Are you all right?"

"Yeah, I'm fine."

They finished lunch, and Charlene told Gary that Josh had asked her to go to dinner that night with an odd, urgent, request. She thanked Gary for letting her understand why. Charlene was the kind of woman that could handle most any situation, especially when it dealt with love, not because she was insightful, but because in the course of her life she had for whatever reasons been exposed to the most bizarre of circumstances. The thing she hated most was being in the dark. When she went to dinner with Josh, she would now understand what he wanted to tell her. Her awareness would make it easier for them both.

Another person might have used the knowledge to let herself grow angry, but not Charlene. Long ago she learned that the only way to survive the white water of life was to follow the river's natural course.

After she left Gary, she decided to take the afternoon off work. Ericson, feeling a little guilty for having cut her feature, gave her no resistance when she told her she wouldn't be coming back in. She drove out to Ocean Beach, parking her car at Sunset Cliffs. Overcast blocked the sun as waves crashed into the rocks far below her. A few cars were parked around her with people drinking or doing drugs. She sighed, and let it sink in what Gary had told her.

Why?

Why did this kind of thing always happen to her? She wondered if there was something really wrong with her personality. She tried to take care of her body. She tried to take care of her mind. Most of the time she felt good about what she had created. Certainly, there were faults with her composure, but even these she felt aware of, and tried to compensate for.

Men would come into her life, and she would fall head over heals in love with them at first. Many times they would end up treating her badly, not physical abuse, but they would be more interested in themselves than in relating with anyone, not just Charlene. With these men she would grow out of love.

Other men would fall in love with her. They would call her, and tell her how wonderful she was. She would look at them, and they would smoke, or they would watch too much television, or they would have an inadequate job and be stressed out by it. They could not even begin to see what Charlene had to offer, and yet they said they loved her. Sometimes, these men would be good enough looking and she would tolerate them to have sex, but she longed for something more.

Then, there were men like Josh. There had not been many of his type in her life. Men that had the potential to be her equal, that could appreciate what was unique about her, but for whatever reason where just a little bit behind her. Maybe they were younger. She was always attracted to the firmness of youth. Or maybe she was just one step ahead. She liked to walk the edge as a trend setter. It's hard to be out in front, and at the same time find someone to stand with you.

She knew that Josh could have been good for her. That he wanted to experience the love of a man, and was willing to attempt it, was something she admired. Not many men are secure enough with themselves to allow for the exploration of those kinds of feelings. Of course, she knew she might loose him. He might come to think of himself as Gay. Maybe he was Gay.

Gary said he always knew that he wanted to be sexual with men. He like women, and occasionally a woman would arouse him sexually, but overall he was most often turned on by men. It was Gary's idea, however, that there really was no such thing as a completely gay, or straight, person, that sexuality was not black and white, but as many different shades of color that could be imagined. Charlene thought that made a lot of sense.

Like a mother watching her child leave home, Charlene had to let Josh live his own life. If anyone was to be her lover, he would have to be her lover, and not have to be forced into it. What is the saying? If you love someone, set them free. If they wish to return to you, you will not have to possess them. Charlene set the whole world free, and found herself very much alone, a lonely soul inside a prison of a needy body.

At the same time her awareness made her sad, the universal truth of her circumstance connected her with ever other lonely soul on this tiny jewel floating in the emptiness of space who searches frantically for someone else's recognition.

Charlene saw herself, and so she saw every other person. A flood of emotion rushed into her. Her heart beat fast, and her skin tingled with energy that flowed from nowhere. Tears gushed like a river from her eyes, but there was not an ounce of self-pity in them. Something touched her and said, "Welcome home." And Charlene wanted to share the feeling with everyone she knew.

Only, everyone she knew was too busy rushing somewhere to hear.

COMING OUT

Josh left Charlene's apartment, angry, that Gary had already told her about their relationship. He jumped into his forest green '59 Chevy pickup, turned on the ignition, it ran poorly, shifted it into gear, and sped off down the road in an unflattering display of machismo that no one was around to see. Josh believed that real man drove impetuously, so as soon as possible, he was right up on someone's bumper, mad as hell that they weren't moving any faster.

Charlene, to her credit, had been understanding, which made Josh's madness even hotter. It hurt his shallow rooted male pride that she gave him up so easily. Of course, he knew he wanted to be with Gary now, though this latest incident of Gary's talking to Charlene without first talking to him, gave him pause for doubt. Still, he had been very much in love with Charlene, and enjoyed how it felt being with her. She was a good woman, and there was no thrill in giving her up, especially, for another man. There was no social support for that kind of switch.

Josh drove down University Avenue, and parked outside Edge, a video bar he frequented on the rare occasions he had the urge to be seen out in public. It was Thursday night, so a kegger was in process, and the bar was hopping. Josh got himself a glass of cheap beer and found a dark spot along one wall where he planted himself to watch the videos and escape from the reality of his so called sordid life.

Unnoticed to him, across the bar sat the always scheming Jacole Smith-Rodriguez with an entourage of his associates from the Project. He, or as they more often say, "she", noticed Josh immediately. The stud was a new face in the bar, or at least one not often seen, and once Jacole got a glimpse of his big arms and what cast a shadow like a meaty basket, true to the inspiration for his name, he began to stalk just like a dog.

That evening Ms. Jacole looked almost normal for a man. He was wearing acid-washed blue jeans and a long sleeve sport shirt, the cuffs rolled up his forearms. A two-day growth of beard sported an illusion of masculinity to his otherwise dough-boyish face. He excused himself to his friends with the pretext of getting himself one last beer while it was still on special. After he filled his cup, he conveniently halted right in front of Josh pretending to look up at the video screen.

"Can you believe that Prince?…He's such a drag queen." The spider Jacole hit on what he hoped to be his next fly.

"I don't know…I kinda like him," quipped Josh. "At least he's his own man."

Jacole was surprised by Josh's tolerance of the rock stars eccentricity. Most "real" men were intimidated by his notorious flamboyance. With a skill at small talk unsurpassed in the city, he continued the conversation, and said, "But don't you think he must be kinda lonely?"

"What do you mean?"

"I mean, who's going to hang around someone that looks like a freak?"

"I don't know. I guess people that admire him for being different, and being a success. He's worth a lot, you know."

"Yeah, Prince is a success, but I tell you, if you tried to do the same thing, you'd just alienate yourself from people. Look at that guy over there with the long hair, Spandex pants, and a halter top or whatever it is he's wearing. He's rocking out to the video, but you notice he's standing there all by himself."

"So."

"So…What do you want out of life? To be alone? Most people want to be with people. And, sad though it may be, to be accepted, you have to sort'a fit in."

"If I wanted to fit in today, I should be styling my hair and shaving my body."

"Well there's different ways to fit in. There's different groups of people to impress. You have to find a group you identify with and then be a little adventuresome, and come out of your closet."

"I don't think I'm in the closet just because I want to be myself."

"But is that what you really want? Or do you want people to like you?"

"What I'd like, if for people to like me being myself."

Jacole laughed at Josh's naivete. When he composed himself, he said, "It just won't happen. If you're too different, you end up threatening people. If you want people to like you, you have to at least make them comfortable when they first meet you."

"Well, that makes sense." Josh finished his beer, and he asked Jacole if he'd like another drink. Jacole, pleased to have weaseled his way into the stud's acquaintance, said he would gladly like another beer. Josh got a beer for his new friend, and a stronger gin and tonic for himself.

As he returned to the dark spot where he felt comfortable, Josh felt the eyes of people upon him. He took a sip of his drink even though it was awkward to drink and walk through the bar at the same time. He thought he needed the booze, but more than that, he needed the activity of drinking, to cut the edge of other people's attention.

Josh was glad Jacole had come up to talk with him. He hated standing by himself in a bar. He didn't like to give people attitude, so he'd try to look at them kindly. But at the same time he didn't always want to give the impression that he was on the make. In fact, the few times he had been to the bar, he never was on the make, because it was too intense, and too public. He wanted to fit in, but maybe Jacole was right, maybe a part of him was afraid to be identified with a people so despised by society at large.

The two men proceeded to get quite drunk. Josh began to forget about Charlene and Gary, not completely, but enough so that he felt more relaxed and had a good time. Jacole wasn't someone he would want to be sexual with, but after a few drinks he seemed witty enough to keep Josh entertained while they were in a bar.

After a while he also turned out to be generous, offering Josh a couple hits of cocaine that they did back in the luxury of a toilet stall. The drug gave them energy which allowed them to reach greater heights of conversation, and stay on their feet when each of their blood alcohol levels should have been enough to knock both of them out.

Josh, feeling different, foolishly, he thought more insightful, said, "I really feel comfortable here."

It was nearly two o'clock in the morning.

"I know what you mean," said Jacole. "Outside the walls of our bars the world hates us, but in here, in here at least we can be ourselves."

"Yeah," Josh agreed, with a drug-forced smile and a plastic shine on his face that came from the reflection of light off of sweat mixed with alcohol and cigarette smoke. "That's what I'm feeling. You know, I'm just now dealing with the fact of being gay. It's not often I feel this comfortable about it."

Jacole consoled, "It takes time to let yourself completely go."

"What do you mean?"

"Well, most of the time when guys come out they can accept, or at least enjoy, the fact they like having sex with men, but they can't integrate that liking into their whole life. They still hide behind a facade of machismo."

"I don't think I'm doing that."

"Sure you are, look at you, and look around you. You dress like some guy from the sticks, your shirt hanging out, your hair unkept, your face oily. Gay men take pride in how they look. That's the first way we judge each other."

Josh complained, "But I've always thought about how I look, and I'm comfortable this way. If someone doesn't like me for that, I'd just as soon not be around them anyway."

Jacole laughed until he choked. "Aw, the luxury of youth. You're lucky you're good looking. Later, you might feel different about it, when your body's old compared to the youth in style, and you have to try a little harder even to get a troll's attention."

Josh was open to what Jacole was saying. After all, he was trying to make a major change in his life. He wanted to experience life as a gay man, and to do what was appropriate for that lifestyle. Maybe he was resisting change by not wearing mousse in his hair. Maybe, he was too self-centered and repressed to adopt a different code of behavior.

All around him it seemed people were having fun, laughing, getting drunk, groping, getting drunker. Two men were dancing on a stage to the fast beat of the quite danceable music. They took off their shirts, revealing fit, if not muscular bodies. They were smiling, and sweating, and totally uninhibited. Josh hoped someday he could be like that.

"To be happy in the gay world," said Jacole, "it's not as important to be your own person, as it is to fit into the crowd."

Josh, finishing his drink, said, "that seems to be true."

"You getting ready to leave?" asked Jacole.

"Yeah."

"Do you mind giving me a lift home? My ride left awhile ago with some number. I just live about a mile from here."

Without a second thought Josh agreed, "No problem."

At the doorway of the bar the men experienced the shock of two worlds colliding head on. San Diego had parts of town where gay people hung out, but no part of town that was exclusively gay. People drove to University from all over the county to get a look at the freaks. They would shout "FAGS!" from their cars and stare. Josh knew many of these men would someday end up on the other end of ridicule. He was ashamed. He knew from experience.

Turning the corner into darkness, the two men walked to Josh's car that was parked in an alley behind the bar. Inside the bar, with its loud music, lights, and energy, they hadn't felt that loaded. But outside, the drink and drugs pushed in the night, and Josh at least was very aware that he was stoned. The combination of speed and liquor, however, gave him a certain control over his movement. He was steady, and he knew he could drive, but he felt different, rather numb.

Suddenly, from somewhere, it seemed out of nowhere, but most likely was from behind a parked car, two men dressed in black appeared as if by magic in front of them to block their way.

"Where do you two faggots think you're going?" said one of the men. At the same time he reached up to hold Josh back, his hand hitting Josh hard in the chest.

It was with this hostile impact that Josh first felt the assault. He did not like being called a fag. The other man pushed Jacole to the ground and proceeded to beat on him. Jacole, or even Josh for that matter, should have yelled, but it was humiliating enough to be beaten up for being gay. Nothing would be worse than to scream like a girl for self defense.

Josh's inaction was short lived, however, because inside of him the hormone adrenaline was being released into his system. His intoxicated state delayed the response, but when it finally came on, it came on like a volcano erupting. Josh was a big man, and all of a sudden he felt very big compared to the two punks beating them up.

In a calm voice that foretold well the storm about to burst upon the scene, he said, "What the fuck do you think you're doing."

"We're cleaning up this town of the likes of you. A.I.D.S. isn't killing you off fast enough."

"I think you better stop it," said Josh still calm.

But then it happened that from the depths of nowhere else but hell an anger moved into his heart that changed the world for him. He saw red. And he saw danger. Then like a man possessed, his body moved quickly, and with certitude in attack of what threatened him. At first the punks resisted, but not for long, because Josh was a maniac. With cunning he laid on his attack, and after bloodying both men considerably, they finally ran off down the alley to nurse their wounds until they found someone a little weaker on whom to take out their revenge.

Josh turned Jacole over, who was lying face down in the dirt. "Are you all right?" he asked.

Jacole's eyes were open, and blood was all over his face from a broken lip. The one punk had been kicking him in the side until Josh ran them off. If one of his ribs wasn't broken, it was severely bruised. He exhaled, "I don't know. I feel pretty sore."

"Try to stand up." Josh lent a hand to his buddy. Cautiously, he stood Jacole up, who after a moment's contemplation decided he wasn't seriously hurt. At least, nothing seemed to be broken.

They walked to Josh's car, which was only a few feet further down the alley, and drove to the Project where Jacole had a small apartment in back. Half way there, the reality of the assault sank in. Josh caught himself trembling uncontrollably. They had been lucky. His mind fantasized about other possible endings to the encounter that left them both dead without anyone being terribly concerned.

The house where Jacole lived was dark. Josh parked the car in the back lot, and the two men walked in through the kitchen.

"Thanks a lot, man," said Jacole, his geniality severely reduced from when they were in the bar. Contributing to his sober mood was the crash from the cocaine they had done earlier.

"You sure you're all right," consoled Josh who had survived the attack much better than Jacole, suffering only a sore hand form where he had hit one of the punks in the face. And that pain soothed his ego, since it was that punch that ran the punks off. Jacole, on the other hand, had been defeated.

"Yeah. It just sort of makes you feel bad to be beat up like that. I'm sure I'll feel better in the morning. I think I just need to get some sleep. Once I forget about it, I'll be all right."

"Okay, I guess I'll be going then," said Josh.

Jacole responded, "Thanks again, friend."

But as Josh was just about to leave, he was delayed to see what looked like a living corpse walking into the kitchen. The skeleton was one of the hospice tenants who had heard the men come in and was coming to get something to drink out of the refrigerator. Jacole greeted him, his name was Jack, and got up to help him despite his bruises and pain.

Jack noticed Jacole's swollen lip, and commented, "What happened to you?"

Coyly, Jacole responded, "Well, Jack, I was playing a little rough tonight."

Jack looked over at Josh, who was big and burly, and also a little roughed up, and then back at Jacole. He nodded his approval that if he were to be beaten up by someone, Josh would be a worthy choice.

Jacole burst out laughing over Jack's fantastic, and silent, summation of the scene. He said finally, "I wish it was in fun, but when we were leaving the bar after a few drinks these punks just laid into us."

Jack suddenly looked sad. He knew that gay bashing had become very popular since A.I.D.S. had reaffirmed being gay as evil again. And he had A.I.D.S., so in some sense he was responsible for his protector's, and that is how he thought of Jacole who was responsible for taking care of him when no one else would, misfortune. It's not like he wasn't suffering enough from being sick. He said, "I'm sorry."

"You're sorry," laughed Jacole. "What do you have to be sorry for? I'm the one that's sorry the whole thing even happened."

Jack answered, "It's because they hate gays that they beat you. And it's because of people like me that they feel justified in hating us all."

"Nonsense," snapped Jacole, glad to have the power to help the helpless, "that kind of thinking doesn't excuse what they do. They're evil, that's all."

Jacole got Jack his paper cup of juice and sent him back to bed.

Josh, waiting for the diseased man to leave, said, "He looked pretty bad."

"It's not a nice way to die, that's for sure," said Jacole. "We have ten of them here now, and it's a lot of work for me to take care of them."

"You do it all alone? Don't you have any help?"

"Well, a few people volunteer, but the Project doesn't have enough money to pay them. We have barely enough to pay a nurse that comes in twice a day. I can understand people not wanting to do this kind of work.

It's not easy taking care of the dying. You know from the start that no matter what you do you will ultimately fail. You have to ignore that, and do what you can day by day."

"Can anyone volunteer?"

"Sure."

"Do you have a card?" asked Josh. "I'll call you."

Jacole gave Josh the phone number, and then Josh left.

On the way home he felt extremely sober, almost depressed. Inside of him feelings were terribly confused. He tried to think about what he was feeling, but no words came to mind that adequately described the sensation of his body. He figured he was just loaded, and gave up trying to make any sense out of what had happened. One thing he knew, though, it was going to be a very rough world being different.

Gary, as usual, arrived at the Gallery just a little past closing time to do his cleaning. It was hot inside the tall plate glass windows of the building's front, and there was fatigue in Gary's movement as he proceeded with his rote ritual of cleaning. Dust-mopping the marble floors, he entered the room where Il Guercino's "Prodigal Son" hung in prominence. He stopped before it, to gaze at his favorite painting. The quiet of the gallery, empty now of tourists and fools, enhanced the soothing energy that flowed between his soul and the work of art.

Inexplicably, he became aware of a presence behind him, an energy that entered the room and was powerful. The sensation caused him to freeze in order to fully experience the feeling. His skin tingled all over, and his cheeks felt like they would explode from the pressure of something inside his body trying to grow beyond the containment of his flesh. Tears welled from his eyes.

The look on the father's face in the painting was so serene, so unconditional. Certainly he was glad for the return of his son, but he did not gloat that his way of life was always better, he took no pleasure in his lost son's remorse. It was cold, hard, selfless love in his gentle touch. And as glad as he might be to have his son return, if the boy should want to leave again tomorrow, the good father would let him go with only the words that he would always be welcome should he desire to come home.

"It is a great painting, isn't it?" said a regal woman's voice with an African accent from behind Gary.

Startled, he turned to see who was intruding. At the same time he asked, "How did you get in here?"

The woman was none other than the same bum he had met the day before in the park. She was his vision. Now, her skin was still black, but her clothes were crisp, clean, and very colorful. On her head she wore a tall hat striped with bands of brilliant orange, yellow, and green.

She answered, "Why, I came in with you."

"But how?" he complained. "I was careful to make sure the door was locked when I came in."

"Yes, I know," she spoke slowly. "You were very careful. But your heart longed to see me. And so, here I am."

Gary noticed how luminous she appeared, her dark skin looked soft like water to touch, and shimmered like water as well. He had an urge to touch her gently, but stayed away leaning on the handle of his mop. The fatigue he had felt earlier was completely gone. He felt suddenly out of time, wide awake with anticipation.

Gary dared to ask the woman her name.

"My name, is Yrba," she said.

"Are you alive?"

"Why? Do I look that bad?"

"No," said Gary, a little embarrassed. "But are you real, or am I dreaming you?"

"Well, I think you came to work, and I think I am here, so I must be real to you. Are you sleeping now?"

"I don't think I've ever felt more awake."

"Most likely that is the truth."

The woman paused. She did not seem to care whether Gary spoke or not. Her eyes were like the father's in the painting, and Gary, like the prodigal son, wanted to turn away from her loving gaze. The steadfastness of her look made him ashamed. How he had wasted his capacity to love that way.

"Why have you come?" he asked her, hoping the facts would place him back in the real time of the world. His stomach felt queasy, like his body was moving faster than his mind. The sensation was becoming uncomfortable.

"I have come to tell you something, something you must share with your brothers and sisters."

No, thought Gary, angels do not come in this day in age. He must be losing his mind to believe the woman before him was anything more than a lunatic street person impersonating divine wisdom. But then, he wondered, why did she speak with such certitude, like she knew who he was, and what he needed?

"Do not be afraid of me, Gary. I do know you, because I am a part of you. I have infected you, and you have made me real in order to understand."

"To understand what?" Gary complained. "I am a simple man trying to make it through life as best I can. Why have you picked me?"

"Are you so simple? Have you not seen the lines of connection in the world? Have you not looked at the stars and wondered?"

"I have felt connected, but in the real world that connection doesn't make sense, or work. Everyone isolates themselves, which works against the flow."

"But you do see the flow."

"I have seen what seems to be the easy way, and have told others, but they resist and never believe me."

"And what happens to them?"

"Sometimes, I can convince them to portage around an impassable stretch of circumstance. And sometimes, I can pull them out of trouble, and save them for a while. But often, they hit the hard places on the side, and then, they drown."

"You are a scout, then."

"But to where? And who am I guiding?"

The regal woman laughed so hard Gary became confused as to what he had said that was funny. When she finally composed, she managed to say, "In time, dear one, in time."

Then Gary felt like something got in his eyes. He rubbed them to relieve the discomfort and when his vision cleared the woman had vanished. He walked all through the gallery to make sure she wasn't hiding out somewhere. He would be in awful trouble if she remained after he locked up for the evening. He even walked around outside the building to see if she was hanging out in the park. But nowhere was she to be found.

After he finished his work, since the sun had not yet set, he took the long way to his car, and walked along the hiking trail that went beneath the tall bridge that connected the two sides of the park across a deep canyon through which a freeway ran into downtown. But on the trail, despite it being so close to the speeding cars, there was a sense of being in the country. At one point, tall pines line the path, at another, a grassy hill. There is even a grove of stately, if still rather small redwoods planted in a side canyon along an exit ramp from the freeway into the park. It was in a clearing of these trees that Gary stopped to think about what was happening to him.

For a long while he had been unhappy with his life, it was true. He often prayed, to what he had no idea, except to put into words the hopes he wished to be fulfilled, that he would find some excitement or purpose in his life. Then he met Joshua, and that should have been the answer. The way they met was certainly a thrill. And his one concern, Charlene, had been understanding. And Josh seemed to genuinely like him. But something else had been happening at the same time, at the exact same time when Gary thought of it. He had had the vision of the woman even as Josh must have been thinking sexually of Gary for the first time.

The vision of Yrba.

What did that woman symbolize to him? His mother? Or something else, something more than a mother, like the Earth herself, like the Almighty Love of God he was taught about as a child. The feminine side of Gary had always felt close to the Earth as Nature. The Earth is like a woman, the fertile ground that gives birth to all that is new. The masculine side of him had planted an idea that maybe, just maybe, he could be something different in this life. Gary wanted to be a part of the world, and not a careless user of it.

But no one was willing to go along with him, and so most of the time he walked alone. Even that day he was alone. No one else seemed to be around in the park. It was getting dark earlier each evening as autumn progressed. Everyone was afraid of the park at night. And perhaps with good reason. The park at night was a lawless place where survival was the rule of order, and death often the outcome of weakness. All around were little shelters littered with an old mattress, a few pages of pornography, and garbage. People lived in these shelters at night, but left them abandoned by the light of day. Gary wondered if his woman slept here at night, if there were others like her in association.

The homeless were an army in rebellion. They lived like guerrillas, warriors against the status quo that had failed to find a niche for them in the scheme of things. Was the woman an emissary approaching him as a member of another disgruntled minority to join together in a militant force of opposition against money, medieval morality, and the failed American dream?

She had said, "I have something to tell you." But then did not say.

Gary got up to move to his car. He thought he saw the shadow of a man move between two trees in front of him. It was only a bird, pecking at the ground for its evening meal. Gary could imagine in his mind what he wanted to become. He could feel it in his body that he was moving in that direction. But he was afraid to tell anyone about it, because what he wanted more than anything was to rest, and that was not a goal his peers admired.

Sitting in his car, as he fastened his seatbelt, he spotted a small but a distinct lesion on his arm he had not noticed before. With a finger he stoked it gently. The spot didn't feel any different that the skin around it. Gary had a notion about what it was, but instead of worrying about it then, he ignored it.

THE REAL PLAGUE

Josh stopped by a liquor store to buy a bottle of red wine Gary asked him to bring over for dinner. Gary was making spaghetti, with a homemade sauce his grandmother taught him to make. Josh wanted to pick a wine that would show his good taste, and decided that if he paid at least ten dollars for a bottle that would guarantee no embarrassment by the label.

Gary's house looked mightily inviting from the street. The lighting was soothing and seductive. Stereo speakers in every room played unusual music, often with signing in a foreign language and style, and rhythm that was just a little different from what would be expected.

In the kitchen was Gary tearing spun-dry lettuce into a bowl. A large pot of salted water was preparing to boil in which to cook the pasta. The rich sauce of chicken and pork with fresh tomatoes, onions, and spice, simmered, filling the room with the smell of a good home, and family. He hollered for Josh to come right on in, and when Josh walked into the kitchen, Gary dried off his hands with a dishtowel, and gave his buddy a big hug, and an affectionate kiss.

"Good to see you," he said, rubbing his friend's strong shoulders and back. To touch Josh rekindled a warmth that had sometimes been distracted during his absence.

Josh, too, was physically stimulated by the contact of their skin. His feelings for Gary had also been mixed since they had seen each other last. Touching again also erased his indifference.

Gary noticed Josh's grimace of pain when he squeezed him tight, and asked, "What's a matter?"

"Oh, nothing."

Josh didn't want to talk about his mugging. To talk about it would mean he'd have to explain why he was out at a bar in the first place.

But Gary was persistent. He said, "Nothing? You're obviously in a lot of pain. How did you get hurt?"

"I'd rather not say," said Josh, not able to look his friend in the eye. "It's a little embarrassing."

"Embarrassing?" Gary's imagination was fired up. Now, he would be satisfied with nothing short of a good story, if not the truth. He begged, "Try me."

Josh was slow to start, but once he began figured he might as well be honest. "Well," he said, "I went out the other night, and on the way out of the bar I got beat up."

Gary was fantasizing more about sex.

He never expected that harm had come to his buddy. His reaction was of concern, and showed no signs of the jealousy Josh feared. He touched Josh lightly and asked, "Are you okay?"

"I seem to be," said Josh acting cool, not admitting the more severe emotional damage the beating had inflicted on him. "I was walking to my car with this guy I met…"

Gary tried to appear expressionless, but a hollowness in his stomach made him painfully aware of the green emotion creeping suddenly inside his heart. He knew he had no right to possess Josh. After all, they hardly knew each other. And he thought it was a good thing Josh was telling him about this other man. That is, rationally he thought it was good. Emotionally, he held his breath for a hopeful explanation.

Josh continued, "Maybe you know him—Jacole Smith-Rodriguez."

"Know him," said Gary with a sigh of relief and a smirk. "I think that queen was the first openly gay person in the city. What was "she" doing talking with you?"

Josh didn't know what to make of Gary's open hostility toward Jacole. He said, "He seemed all right to me. He was very sensitive to how I was feeling."

"I'm sure he was very sensitive." Gary laughed. "But what happened to you guys?"

"Really, there's not much to tell. After we left the bar, these guys jumped us. At first, I panicked, but as soon as my wits came to me, I guess I scared them off."

"Well, I'm glad you weren't hurt too bad. Is Jacole all right?"

"Yeah. I gave him a ride home. You know he lives at the A.I.D.S. Project."

"Really?"

"I think it's very generous, him helping those guys out."

Gary went back to working on the dinner. He said, "Probably he's guilty about his past."

"What do you mean?" asked Josh.

Gary stirred the pasta into the hot water.

"Well," he answered, "Jacole might not have anything to be guilty of personally, but in the past, and not so distant past I've heard, your friend Ms. Rodriguez was the epitome of gay decadence. Now, she wants to be Mother Teresa."

Josh didn't like Gary's sarcastic tone. He complained, "That doesn't seem fair."

Gary was short to respond in a somewhat angry voice, "Tell that to the people she's exploited in the past that are dead."

Josh wasn't looking to start an argument so early in the evening, or their relationship for that matter, so he backed off a bit, and conceded, "Well, I only talked to him one night. He seemed nice enough, but I suppose you can't really tell."

"It's not that important," also aware that an argument over the merits of Jacole hardly mattered. "I'm acting like your mother."

They both laughed because Josh said that Gary would have made a lot better mother than he actually had. He could not remember seeing so much good looking food being prepared as a child. He commented, "Don't you think you're going a little overboard with the food?"

Gary replied, "I've invited a few other friends over. I think you'll like them."

"Then give me a cork screw for this wine," said Josh. "I don't think I'm quite ready to meet them cold sober."

The first to arrive that evening was Charlene, which would seem like an awkward thing, given that Josh and she had never really talked about their relationship since the world had changed. When she heard Gary was making dinner she had insisted on coming. And to make the evening even more dynamic, as was her nature without malice, she came with Gary's ex-lover, though still a good friend, Philip. The first few seconds after their arrival, which was not really as a couple, was somewhat strained, that is, until Charlene very skillfully reduced the level of tension by giving Joshua a big hug in greeting, and after kissing him, the playful reprimand, "You naughty, naughty, boy."

Josh felt like he had moved onto Payton Place, the interconnection between these four people too bizarre for the comfort appropriate to a good dinner party guest list. But the others didn't seem to mind, so why, he thought, should he?

For Gary's part, he had not seen Philip for a few weeks, and was glad that Charlene had thought to include him in the festivities. It was more than two years since they had stopped living together, and their relationship in the mean time had actually grown more supportive than when they were always at each other's throats.

Philip said, "Great music, Gar."

"It's Baaba Maal."

"Never heard of him."

"From Senegal."

"Guess that's why," said Philip with a smirk. He probably knew Gary better than anyone. "You always are so progressive."

"This is an old album, friend. I only just heard about it."

"Hey," said Charlene. "What kind of hosts are you guys? What about some wine for your guests?"

Josh grabbed the bottle. Charlene opened the cupboard and got out two glasses.

As Josh poured the wine in Philip's glass, Philip caught a glimpse of the label. He unconsciously complimented the wine, "Sarducci, that's a nice wine."

Gary, noticeably gloating to someone in tune, said, "Josh, brought it."

To Josh, Philip tipped his glass, "Good choice."

Josh was relieved to find it true that if you're willing to pay the right price you don't need to know anything about class to be sophisticated. He rolled with it, "It's just a little something I thought you all might like."

Philip acknowledged that he did like it with a raise of his eyebrow, not only over the wine, but the hunk of a man who brought it.

It did not pass over Charlene, Philip's obvious enthrallment with Josh as a specimen of masculinity. She took a gulp of what she thought was a rather ordinary wine, chuckling to herself. She asked Gary, "Are we it?"

Gary, who was facing away from her, now moved on to preparing a homemade vinegarette, said, "No dear. I've invited a few other people, a couple of them from the gallery you might be interested in."

"Jorgensen?" she asked with anticipation.

Gary turned around smiling.

Charlene rushed over to him and gave him a big kiss. "You dog! He doesn't know I work for the paper does he?"

"No way! Do you think I'm stupid?"

"No, but you know how important it would be for me to get an interview with him."

"Well, be tactful please. No one's supposed to even know he's in town. He seems very nice. The director had me driving him around today, and despite his prominence in the art world, he's about as regular as you could expect."

"God!" exclaimed Charlene, revealing her enthrallment with the world famous, very young, director of the National Cultural Institute. "He's so important. It just goes to show you how fake most people's snobbish attitudes are."

"When I told him I was making homemade spaghetti, he insisted on coming."

Charlene squeezed Gary's cheek. "They always say the way to a man's heart is through his stomach. Leave it to you, Gary."

Sonary Jorgensen was one of America's renegade philosophers, and self-taught critic of art. Frequently in print, it was almost impossible to get a personal interview with him, since he was always concerned that his casual word would be misrepresented. Of course, for his notoriety, this aloofness was indispensable. The further he removed himself from the public, the more he was dutifully worshiped.

The Director of the Timken had asked Gary to drive Sonary around while he was in town, and the two men hit it off almost immediately. Gary was more than intelligent enough for the scholar, who found most of his peers credentialed boors. And more important perhaps, Gary appeared to be a spirit working toward freedom, something Sonary found inspiring.

Jorgensen suspected Gary's homosexuality almost immediately—a good-looking man willing to talk about art before women, who would not suspect? And despite the fact he was long married to a notorious elitist bitch, he was not above an occasional walk on the wild side for a little fun, and he soon began to tease Gary to see how far he could get, most hopefully into his pants.

Jorgensen's advances, however, made Gary uncomfortable. Though playing coyly had so far worked to keep the celebrity scholar at bay. Gary hoped Sonary was nothing more than a harmless tease whose leash had been let out too far, and decided to use his desirability to his superior advantage in order to help Charlene score a journalistic coup. Maybe if the philosopher liked her, she could get an interview. In any event, she would get to know him in a relaxed situation which was valuable in itself, something that had not escaped the reporter.

Gary added as he stirred the sauce, "I think he's coming with a woman named Mary Swanson, who's someone he knows from the University."

"Do you know her?" asked Philip.

"No," said Gary. "Just that she teaches philosophy there, and is a friend of his."

"Philip," Gary changed the subject. "Could you please take the salad out to the dining room?"

Philip, who was well trained to assist Gary from their years of living together, set down his glass of wine that was nearly empty and reverted to an old routine that was a part of being with Gary he had always enjoyed.

The door bell announced a guest.

Charlene, obviously excited, even letting out a pip of a squeak, nervously said, "That must be him. Can I get it?"

"Sure," said Gary as he continued stirring the sauce. "But try to let him feel at home a bit, before you eat him alive." Then, he laughed.

Charlene, with the coyness of a brat whose cute behavior had been made transparent, made a funny face and responded, "I know how to act in public, thank you."

"Yeah," said Gary still laughing. "I know exactly how you act."

Charlene adjusted her clothes and catching a glimpse of herself in a mirror above the mantel in the living room, her hair. She opened the door to see the famous Jorgensen in blue jeans with his escort who looked like a doughty old maid with a chiseled face and eyes that didn't quite seem to be focused in the here and now.

"Good evening," she greeted them. "You must be Sonary Jorgensen and Mary Swanson."

"That's right," said Sonary.

"Gary's in the kitchen. I'm Charlene Dice. Won't you please come in."

As he entered, Sonary took Charlene's hand and kissed it gently. "Glad to meet you."

It's not often a girl is swept off her feet in California, but Sonary's old world elegance and Charlene's suppressed romantic needs despite a veneer of self-reliance, resulted in the modern woman swooning, obviously.

Gary entered the room, just in time to see Charlene's "disgraceful" display of womanliness which he acknowledged with a slight raise of his eye she witnessed, to greet his distinguished quests. Introductions were made to all, and Philip poured the newcomers each some wine. Then, they all moved into the living room to sit down to a round of conversation before eating.

Charlene began the talk in a manner that almost got her pulled from the room to help Gary bring in the appetizers. She asked Sonary without the slightest masking, or warming up, "Do you think it wise for a city like San Diego to make the attempt to popularize fine art for the masses?"

Sonary was used to having to give his opinion often about such matters, so in a way, it would have been more awkward for Charlene to ask him a question about, say, his day. Gary saw in his face no malice or discomfort for being put on the spot. So he let Charlene go, though, not without giving her a glance of rebuke that she noticed warning her to be careful.

Sonary responded quite diplomatically, "I don't think it's ever unwise to make the attempt to educate people." He leaned toward Charlene. "Do you have a specific example in mind?"

"Not really," said Charlene, gulping a swallow of wine. "I don't know if Gary told you, but I work for the paper and I was just curious about your general feelings about the Chinese Arts Festival."

"Oh," said Sonary. "Gary didn't tell me you worked for the paper."

Gary shook his head and made a grimace chastising Charlene's lack of restraint despite having been warned. Mary Swanson, however, was the one to defuse the situation, even though she knew nothing about anyone in the room. She said, "Oh, Sonary, don't be so taken aback. The young girl's interest should flatter you."

"Well," he said sarcastically, "it might flatter me if her interest was over something other than my opinion."

"But, Sonary," joked Gary, "you're a married man. That kind of attention could get you into trouble."

"Oh, yeah, that's right," he said. "I forgot. I'm married."

The lustful twinkle in his eyes as he addressed himself to Gary made the good-looking host uneasy. He reduced his stress by quickly leaving the room to get more wine and some cheese and water biscuits. Josh followed him to help.

Sonary continued, "Now that would be a good discussion: what the hell marriage means?" He turned his attention to Mary. "And we're lucky enough to have a working philosopher with us. What do you think of that question, Mary?"

"I think you should have another glass of wine, Sonary, and relax?"

"Mary?"

"You know very well I'm in no mood to discuss relationships."

"Oh, that's right, I forgot." Then, he turned his attention to Charlene and Philip. "Mary thinks she's doomed to be an old maid. She just turned forty-five, with no love interest in sight."

Charlene immediately put on a mask of sympathy. She was sure Miss. Swanson must have been a good philosopher. With looks like hers, she thought, she probably had no trouble finding time to read. She said, however, "Mary, you never know when love will show up. Though in my life it's when I'm looking for it that it's always the scarcest."

Mary laughed, causing Charlene to become a little resentful. She could have been more honest, and was sure Mary would then have found a lot less to find amusing. But Mary explained, "I'll tell you what's important to me. It's not the love of a stupid man that's going to do whatever he wants anyway. For me, the true ecstacy of love is getting to know the great minds that have lived on this planet. Like Immanuel Kant for instance, now there was a man."

"No offense, Mary," quipped Charlene, "but I think he's been dead for some time. I doubt his touch would be very stimulating."

"Dear, if that's all you're looking for," returned the scholar, "you'd be better off going to the store and buying you something made of plastic you can rely on."

Philip exploded in laughter. It seemed the "old maid" had a wit to her, and balls to speak so honestly to people she only just met. He found her becoming more attractive. Joining the conversation, he said, "Now, Mary, not all men are bad."

"Yeah," added Sonary.

"Well," she changed her tune, "present company excepted." Though she still was rather sardonic. "Most men would find more than an adequate match in a dildo. Now, a man like Kant, there was someone willing to take the chance to be different. You know he set free the mind for all the technological advances we have today, because he dared to release the religious mind from the shackles of irrational dogma."

"Grand words, Swanson." Sonary spoke with a snobbish accent and applauded her. "Remind me next time to brush up on the history of philosophy before I invite you to another party."

"You know, you make fun of me, but even though people don't know the names of these great thinkers, their ideas are still influenced by them."

"No doubt," said Sonary, "and I'm not making fun of you."

Then that present got a taste of his ability to lecture.

"But I'd object that the thoughts of great philosophers like Kant have done only good for our world. In fact, I sometimes wonder more about the effect of lesser people on this planet. Just last week I was in Seattle taking the ferry across Puget Sound and I thought, how beautiful this place is. And yet even there, in the midst of all that beauty, hardly a spec of the land has not in some way been altered by our species. The forests are all young and in rows, and everywhere there are homes and factories, manicuring the planet, and often polluting it. I have a friend there who is dying of A.I.D.S. And I want to somehow understand how disease is not destruction so that his suffering might be less tragic. We all believe what we do in life is improving the planet, whether we are developer or environmentalist.

Though at the same time we are ourselves like a virus weakening the Earth that supports us. No malice can be ascribed to our action, because we cannot know what we are doing. Like HIV, we are just living our nature. And like HIV, it seems we too are a plague."

Out in the kitchen, Josh and Gary couldn't hear the conversation. Gary opened another bottle of wine, while Josh arranged the cheese and crackers on a plate.

Josh said, "These people make me feel uncomfortable."

"Just relax," Gary comforted. "It's just a different style. You'll get used to it."

"But I haven't been to school. I don't know anything about art, or philosophy."

"But you look good. For you, it doesn't matter. They'll all want to know you anyway."

"Huh?"

"Bottom line always, is how you look. If you're young, and in style, they pay attention to you. The only education you need then, is to be smart enough to take advantage of that. If you do, you'll go far."

"Far, until they catch on to you and drop you for the next guy."

"Well, hopefully by then you've made something for yourself."

"Ah, so that's the key…selfishness."

"Not selfishness, self-interest. There's a difference."

"For a philosopher to distinguish, I'm sure."

They both laughed. Gary said finally, "Tonight, it doesn't matter anyway. We're throwing the party. They'll be nice to us because they want to eat." Then, they walked back to feed the others.

In the living room Philip was discussing how he became dissatisfied with being a homosexual, and how now he was looking for the right woman to please him. Philip was near forty, with thinning hair. He had been a school teacher until he left that profession to explore his feelings for other men. Also, he didn't like being told what he was to teach his kids.

He taught social studies and got into a lot of trouble one year when he
had his eighth grade class read excerpts from Marx's "Communist
Manifesto." The administration said that the work was not appropriate.
Philip was trying to explain to his class how democratic reform in
Communist countries was consistent with Marx's idea of socialism. It dis-
illusioned him to realize education had little to do with learning, and so
he went into business with a friend who restored old houses for a profit.

In the early eighties there was good money to be made in real estate,
and Philip did well for himself and was glad to be away from being told
what to do by others. During that time he met Gary, and had a pretty
good relationship with him, until sex got old and he was frightened by the
possibility of getting A.I.D.S. One day he went to get tested for the virus'
infection, and when he found out he was negative he decided to stop having sex with men. When this all happened it drove Gary crazy, who could
not so easily turn off his sexual interest in someone he loved. But finally,
after a year of strained living, Philip moved out to live his new life, and
seemed happy. And Gary became happier with himself, and for his friend
in time.

Philip was saying, "…people should just accept that sexuality is not any
one way. Sexual energy flows from the body, and should be expressed in
whatever way is appropriate for the time."

Gary, embarrassed, broke in, "More wine for anyone?"

All the glasses moved forward to be refilled.

Charlene, continued with Philip's thought, "I don't think people have
to accept it. The body will do what it wants. If the brain can't accept it,
they'll just be guilty." She was thinking of Josh.

"Ah, guilt!" said Sonary. "You must have been raised Catholic."

Charlene laughed. "Why, yes."

"It's a pleasure to be around someone else who sees evil everywhere in
the world."

Gary, remembering all the times Charlene got drunk and rather wild, said, "But not much fear of evil, it seems only enough to make bad behavior more enticing."

"What do you expect from a bunch of sexually frustrated men, living in supposed poverty surrounded by some of the grandest luxury the earth has ever known?"

"I don't know how sexually frustrated they were," said Mary. "I've heard there's quite a collection of Greek and Egyptian's pornographic art in the Vatican."

"Really?" asked Josh.

"Yes," said Mary. "Of course, it's never mentioned, like the hundreds of other things stashed away *we* would be better off not knowing about."

"Imagine that," said Philip, "the Pope himself getting off looking at some statue of an old man plowing some young stud."

"Philip!" chastised Charlene.

"It's just a thought, Charlene. I don't see how *that* can hurt anyone."

Gary said, "They say it's thoughts that will send you to Hell before action."

"Ah, to hell with Hell," Philip responded disgusted. "I'm gonna go to Hell anyway for plenty of other things I've done in this life. I only hope, and completely expect, that the people I like will be there with me so I don't have to spend an eternity down on my knees in front of some worship-starved deity."

Gary couldn't resist making fun of his ex-lover's change of sexual orientation, "Oh, that's right. Perhaps, if the deity was a woman you'd rise to the occasion."

Charlene giggled, because she knew Gary meant the comment in fun, and also, because she had seen Philip do just that. Gary looked at her, and she blushed wondering if he suspected.

Sonary moved the conversation along on its difficulty of five white water flow. "How about that Voyager?"

Josh did not much like talking about sex, but space he liked. He said, "I watched some of the pictures come down. It was really quite remarkable. And I don't mean the science, I mean how it affected my imagination to think I was somehow that far out in space."

Mary agreed, "The pictures, even before they were enhanced, were spectacular."

But Charlene had another view, "I don't see what all the fuss is about. It's a ball of gas so far away it doesn't have any influence on us. The project was a good deal I suppose. They always say so on the news. I just can't get into it."

"But it does influence us," said Sonary in a somewhat condescending tone, like a father might use with an air-head child. "Look at Triton, for example. There's a world so cold we would have expected, because of what we experience here, that it would be solid as a rock. I heard it was twenty-seven degrees Kelvin, twenty-seven degrees above absolute zero, where nothing is supposed to move. That number may be wrong, but if it's true, think of it. Twenty-seven degrees above when nothing should move, there is not only a world in motion, but one of the most interesting in the solar system."

Josh joined Sonary's excitement, "I know! When you look at it, you wonder if it wouldn't be possible to have a life totally different from what we know, in a world like that."

Gary felt a buzz of electricity move across his forehead.

"No way," said Philip. "I saw the pictures, it's beautiful, but nothing could live there."

Gary interrupted the conversation, "Charlene, come help me finish the dinner. It'll be about five minutes 'till we eat."

"Great!" exclaimed Philip as they left. "I'm starving."

Mary, now a little more relaxed after several glasses of wine, turned her attention onto Josh, who she thought was rather attractive, even more so because he had been so quiet. She said, "Josh, you haven't said much."

Josh, nervously replied, "I'm not one for dinner parties."

The others laughed.

He continued, "I mean, I don't know what to talk about. I don't have an interesting job, and haven't gone to college. I go to the gym, work to pay my bills, and am usually too tired at night to do any profound thinking."

Sonary, amused, said, "I wouldn't always call what I do profound."

"Others would," said Philip.

"Yes, I know," said Sonary. "But then, that's their problem, isn't it."

"I suppose. But you must admit, once you gain a little reputation, you can ride that for quite a way in this world."

"Oh yes, that's true, that's very true. I think I did my greatest work when no one knew me, when most people I talked to just thought I was just crazy for being interested in anything other than making money."

"It seems you've always been famous," said Mary. "Was there really a time when people didn't know you?"

"It's hard even for me to remember, but yes, I can remember quite well wondering whether it was worth pursuing a career in philosophy."

"But it paid off for you," said Josh.

"What paid off, dear boy, was sticking with it. It was patience and perseverance that paid off, not anything I thought of, or supposedly created. It's a weird world. There are many people thinking as great of thoughts I could ever imagine, perhaps you are even one of them, but for whatever reason, their lives don't allow them to exist as thoughtful people long enough to be noticed by society. As a result, we believe only a few people are fit to think, while the rest of us must blindly accept what they believe. I tell you, that's bullshit."

Gary called from the dining room, "Dinner's ready."

Josh protested, "But, Sonary, is it really possible for a person like me, who has no education outside of a vocation, to be taken seriously by someone like you?"

Sonary, in true philosophical form answered Josh with the question, "What is it about a person that should be taken seriously?"

Mary suggested, "Surely, not their education."

"Well, an education can help."

Philip jumped in, "When I try to think about the one characteristic I find common to all of my friends, and I have many different kinds of friends, it is that they all are honest."

"Ah, honesty!" exclaimed Sonary.

"The greatest virtue," Mary proclaimed, "at least, in this day in age."

"Honesty?" queried Josh. "And how do you tell someone's honest?"

Gary just then walked into the room. He said, "I don't know how to tell someone's honest, Mr. Socrates, but I can tell you when a cook is about to get upset because a dinner's getting cold and no one's coming over to eat it."

They didn't wait for an answer. The table looked spectacularly appetizing. Once everyone was in their seat Gary proposed a toast. "To good conversation, and good food: the spice of life."

Everyone agreed, and after the sound of clinking glass the room was rather quiet except for an occasional moan of ecstacy over the taste of the food. Charlene was the most audible, until Philip, sitting next to her, commented in fun, "Charlene, you're making me hot!"

Everyone burst into laughter, Gary choking when he swallowed wrong. Charlene turned bright red, but had to admit that eating a good meal did have a quality to it that resembled good sex. Looking straight at Josh she said, "And since I haven't been getting any of the later recently, I guess I'll just have to take my satisfaction when I can."

"Here, here," said Sonary. "It is a dry time for getting regular sex."

Gary returned, "Well, I don't think it would be wise to be as free as we once were." He thought of his friend Joe in the hospital.

"Certainly not!" agreed Mary. "I get as horny as the next person, but quite frankly, sex scares me to death."

Philip couldn't help thinking, sex probably would no doubt scare anyone she was with to death as well.

Josh felt this was a subject he could comment on without feeling inadequate. He said, "I don't think it's sex, that's scary. It's just that people seem to deny the existence of any danger with it."

Gary thought Josh's comment interesting. Wasn't it Josh, who always pushed for unsafe sex? Of course, he claimed to be negative, and that made it all right.

Charlene, also irritated by Josh's comment, since it was exactly that kind of rationale by a bisexual that was the greatest threat to straight society, said with a little resentment, "But I think it's exactly your placing of the word danger next to sex that's causing the problem. That's what makes denial easy when you get into passion."

"Huh?" said Josh, partly not understanding Charlene's point, partly picking up on her very subtle hostile tone.

"I mean that it's easy to think about the danger of having unsafe sex when you're not wanting to fool around. But when you're really passionate, and I know that even in these progressive eighties it's still not easy to talk openly about this, I mean, really wanting to get it on, you've got to admit that emotion takes over your body and reason doesn't work so well. Sex is fun! And you can call it dangerous as often as you like, but remember who you're telling it to. Your telling it to people who like to smoke, drive fast cars, and drink and drug themselves under the table for fun. That death is associated with it makes it all the more attractive."

"Aw, Charlene," cautioned Gary, "Calm down. This is hardly the time for a diatribe against modern morality."

Mary, in support of Charlene's message, said, "I think she's very insightful, sobering, yes, but still very insightful."

Charlene continued, "I'm not trying to be negative. But I think people deceive themselves when they don't admit that the whole problem of A.I.D.S goes far beyond staying alive."

Josh, now definitely offended, said, "By people, do you mean me?"

"Get over yourself, Josh. By people, I mean people in general, myself included, who don't want to honestly examine how they feel about sex and love enough to grow beyond our present understanding of what such an animal urge can mean to us."

Sonary, obviously impressed by Charlene, said, "Intriguing! I've never thought about it that way. I mean, I've never thought about how the current crisis might allow us to finally integrate our emotions with the advances that reason has made over the last two thousand years."

"Oh, Sonary," chuckled Mary, "You are such a romantic. People are dying hideous deaths, and all you can think about is how it will help the age of reason."

"Mary, I can feel for those people, but there's really nothing I can do about them being ill. Feeling sorry for them, surely won't help them any. I think Charlene is on to something when she says we have pushed our true feelings about sex down because of the present situation."

"That's not surprising," said Philip. "Just think about it. In the sixties everyone was so excited to be liberated from the stuffy and repressive morality of the Victorian era. I'm sure behavior didn't change much, but for the first time people were able to openly express themselves sexually. In the seventies that expression was taken to the extreme, especially by the homosexuals. Then, in the eighties, BANG, the plague. We should have seen it coming, not because it's the wrath of God, but because we should have known that morality originally evolved for a reason. Sometime in the past, surely people must have realized that promiscuous sex led to disease, not because that sex itself is bad, but because part of being human on this planet puts us at risk to disease. We are not the only living things trying to survive. The sun doesn't shine just for us. Bacteria and viruses also have a right to survive, and as it turns out, human sex provides a good way for them to move around."

Josh broke in, "So we should just die so a one celled creature can live and multiply?"

"No!" objected Philip. "Before, we had no science to understand what was going on with disease. People had a lot of sex, they got sick, and died, so, of course, it appeared that sex was the cause. But now we know, or at least, we should know better. A virus is the cause. It's Science's project to find a treatment for that. But it's our project, the healthy's project, to understand something new about sex that will help us not only love each other safely, but in the best way that's ever been possible up to now."

Everyone sat in silence, thinking over Philip's point.

Gary broke their reflection, "Well, Charlene, your moans really got us going, but I don't think we're going to solve this problem tonight. Come on, and help me bring in dessert."

Charlene and Gary left to cut up a blueberry cheesecake, and make some coffee. The others helped to clean up the table. Sonary and Mary even did some of the dishes, since Gary's house didn't have a dishwasher. Everyone talked cordially, with the conversation becoming much more mundane.

It grew late, and since it was a week night, around ten thirty Mary and Philip excused themselves. Shortly thereafter, Sonary and Mary also left. Gary put on an ambient CD by Brian Eno, lit the candles over the mantle in the living room, and lay down on the couch. Josh finished washing the dishes, and swept the dining room floor of the crumbs.

He said as he worked, "It was a good dinner, Gary."

"Thanks. I hope everyone had a good time."

"They seemed to. I'm not used to talking like they do, but even I had a good time. The food was great."

"Charlene seemed upset."

"Yeah, I think she's mad at me."

"I don't know. She says she is okay about us being together."

"I know. But still I think she's a little resentful."

"I wonder if she and Philip are fooling around?"

Josh was silent.

"Does that bother you?"

"No. I hadn't really thought about it though."

"Well, you know he's a straight man now. I wouldn't put it past Charlene to deal with us by catching one coming the other direction. She says men who explore homosexuality are more sensitive."

"Really? Is that so?" Josh put down the broom and moved over to lay next to Gary. "I don't know if sensitive is the best word to describe what I'm feeling." He pushed up hard against Gary.

For some reason Gary was uncomfortable with Josh's advance. He didn't feel sexual, or was afraid to be sexual. So much was happening to him. He thought about telling Josh about the woman in the Gallery, but then, decided not to. There was a quality to her appearance that scared him, and made him think he was losing his mind. And then there was his lesion. He felt unclean. Gary pushed Josh away, just slightly.

"What's wrong?"

"I don't know." Gary paused. "I think we should use a rubber when we have sex."

"All right," said Josh, like all of a sudden it wasn't an issue. "Any reason for the sudden concern? We both are negative."

"Well, I think I'm negative, but you know I've never been tested. And you say you've never been with men before so chances are you're safe."

"And you said you never got fucked regularly, especially since you knew it was unsafe. But if you'd feel better we'll just use a rubber."

"I would."

"And maybe we both should get tested. I'll ask Jacole."

"Jacole?"

"Yeah, I guess I didn't tell you. I've volunteered to work at the Project a couple nights a week."

DEMENTIA

*S*everal weeks later, Josh got up early to get ready for work. Gary rose with him and made some freshly ground coffee, an African blend, while Josh took a shower. The two men then sat out on the back deck, high among the branches of a California pepper tree. They talked in whispers out of consideration for others still sleeping, and enjoyed a warm still morning of the Southern California Fall.

In other parts of the country it is the crispness in the air that signals the change of seasons. But in the Southland the change is more subtle. The warm air of the Santa Ana winds combined with the steep angle of September light make autumn a surreal time of year, when nature seemed almost perfect and kind, not at all foretelling the harshness of winter she was about to unfurl on the unsuspecting. Fall in California is a time of possibility, and, for those open to it, love.

Josh sat up close to his buddy, like a dog to the one who feeds it. His eyes drooped dependence, which would normally disturb Gary, because he had learned long before how dangerous it can be to rely on someone else. Only through self-reliance is there stability, but Gary thought, maybe he had become too jaded to enjoy the pleasure of being in love with another.

Josh gazed into Gary's eyes. He said, "You know, every day I feel closer to you. It's like the ground beneath my feet just dropped away and I'm floating."

Gary laughed. "You're twenty-eight years old, and you talk like you're falling in love for the first time."

"Maybe, I am." Josh gently caressed the hair on Gary's forearm. "I think about you constantly. At first, I was scared to let my feelings go, but now that I know you care about me too, it's like I've been overcome."

"Be careful."

"I don't want to be careful. I just want to be around you."

Gary kissed his friend softly. "It's wonderful. You're like a child."

"I'm the luckiest man in the world. I live in a time when I can be myself, and I've found someone I can play with."

"Yeah, babe. You sure can play with me."

Josh got a look in his eye that said he wanted to play right then.

Gary questioned, "Won't you be late for work?"

"My work," said Josh between kisses, "will still be there."

After Josh left, Gary made the bed, straightened up the bathroom, and started to water his house plants, which were very dry from neglect. He brought them one by one out onto the deck and was watering them with the garden hose when he thought he heard the sound of the door bell.

Checking the door, though, no one was there, so he continued his work.

But a few minutes later he again heard what sounded like knocking. By looking through a back window he could see the front door. Still, no one was there.

That's odd, he thought. He then walked through the house, out onto the front porch. Looking down the street in both directions, he saw it was deserted. He thought that maybe the Jehovah Witnesses where out campaigning. They were usually the only ones to come by so early unannounced.

He then walked back inside, and straightened the magazines on the coffee table. Through the corner of his eye he thought he caught a glimpse of a shadow moving in the hallway. His heart began to beat faster as he walked cautiously to inspect. But the hallway was empty. And after checking both bedrooms, and their closets, not a thing was to be found.

Gary rubbed his face and eyes, and took a deep breath. It made him uneasy to think someone was watching him. Was he getting paranoid?

Then, as if nature thought fit to answer his question, while he still had his eyes covered, he was startled to hear the soft voice of a woman call out his name. It sounded like she was standing out front.

Gary ran back outside, but still could see no one. He called out, "Where are you?"

This time, from back inside the house, he heard the answer, "Why, I'm in here."

Gary turned around to see something he wished more than anything to be only a dream. There in his living room stood a most remarkable sight. A young girl, blond, and with a thin white dress flowing away from her, floated just above the floor with her arms outstretched in invitation to embrace him. Gary walked slowly over to her raising his hand to touch her wet voluptuous lips. But just when he was about to feel their warmth, she vanished into thin air.

From behind him a courser female voice began to laugh hysterically. He turned to see the black woman from the park bent over a chair, obviously enjoying herself.

He asked in an irritated voice, "How'd you get in here."

As soon as she stopped laughing, which was not for some time, she said, "Why, man, I walked through the front door. How else you gonna get inside?"

"But how did you know where I lived?"

She stood silent. Changing the subject, she asked, "Got anything to eat?"

"Eat? Who the hell do you think you are busting in here wanting something to eat?"

She made a pouting face. "How much can it hurt you to help me? I'm hungry...I'm hungry for your food."

"Why don't you get a job, then?"

"I can pay you."

"With what?"

"What do you need most?"

"Huh?"

"I say, what is it that you need most?"

Her manner suggested that she was indeed able to pay in any manner Gary could accept. But he knew, as he watched her fumble through the pages of a magazine only looking at the pictures, that she was nothing more than a park bum. Reaching into his pocket he took a five-dollar bill from his wallet and handed it to her, saying, "Here, take this, and go buy yourself something to eat. And make sure it's not booze!"

"Why, thank you." She took the bill, folding it several time, and placed it in the front pocket of her jeans. "But why should you worry how I spend it?"

"Liquor's not good for you."

"Not good? Not good for me! Oh, you are kind, most kind to be concerned."

"All bums are drunks. Everyone knows that."

"Are they? Like all fags are…"

"Now, wait a second, who you calling a fag?"

"I wasn't callin' no one anything. I was just making a point." She smiled, her big white teeth looking something like the Cheshire cat as he was about to disappear.

Gary acknowledged, "I suppose, one well taken."

The woman became animated. She said excitedly, "Here, I must give you something to show my thanks."

"There's no need of that," assured Gary. "Just take the money and go."

"But Gary…"

"How do you know my name?"

She stood up and walked over to him. Face to face, she said, "Your name is Gary Nolan. You work, very little to your credit, as the janitor of the Timken Art Gallery. You are lonesome, and believe there is something wrong with that. You are in love…but at the same time, you are very afraid of losing your way."

"But how?" asked Gary, somewhat fearful she could know so much.

"You said it. I'm a bum. What else does a bum have but time to find these things out."

"No—A bum would not be interested. Why are you so interested?"

"Actually, I'm interested in a lot of people, but no one listens to me. You are special, but no better than the rest. You're special because you can hear. Don't you remember calling for me?"

Gary shook his head to signify that he had no idea what she was talking about. But he did know that he had very explicitly prayed to be recognized. Could this woman have come in answer to his prayer? He wanted badly to believe that even in this day of technology, miracles could still happen, but then why a bum, why not the angel he had seen earlier, and expected?

The black woman laughed and laughed at his indecision. She knew from the look on his face that he was confused. "You're lying!" she said. "I remember it well. I was looking down on you. You were sitting on your back deck watching a small fire burn in that Mexican fireplace that looks like a bandit. And you prayed, because you were lonely then."

Gary's mouth fell open in amazement.

"And after I came down—you saw me as a falling star—to be with you."

Breaking her hypnotic stare, Gary turned toward the mantle, and said, "No. I won't hear this; you can't possibly know that happened."

"You're right!" she said without a fight. "I can't possibly know what's written on your face so clearly that anyone not blind can see. Can I help it if you live in a world of darkness? This planet spins too far away from the sun to make the obvious transparent."

"This planet?"

"Oops!" She placed her hand over her mouth. "Did I say *this*?" She became over dramatically cute, "I meant, our."

Gary in a very serious tone said, "You meant what you said: I can tell. Are you some kind of an alien?"

Yrba turned hostile, "What does it matter to you? You work for Immigration? You want to deport me?"

"I don't mean that kind of alien," said Gary. "You're from another world, aren't you?"

"Ain't that the truth," she said sarcastically. Looking around the room, she added, "And a good thing, too, from the looks of this place. Too many knickknacks. Too many things cluttering up the soul."

"Then where do you come from?" asked Gary, now obsessed.

"Where do you come from?" she responded as she slowly circled Gary. "So many memories protect you, it's hard to see the core of what you are." She lifted her hands and placed them on either side of Gary's head, not touching him, but feeling for the energy he emitted.

"What are you doing?" he asked.

"People. A group of people, around you. Laughing. Talking. You are the center of attention, young, in a new car, and a new face at your gym. Everyone gathers around to be your friend, you think."

"None of them are my friends."

"But it felt like friendship then. What was it?"

"It was a waste of time. I always felt lonely." Gary stepped back from Yrba. "How can you be so sensitive to me?"

"Because I am your conscience."

"No: You are a park bum," he snapped. "But you do seem to know an awful lot about me."

Yrba looked hurt. Then, in a more serious tone she said simply, "The truth then: I was sent to help you make sense."

Her words upset Gary. He pulled at his hair and shouted, "What is there, that needs to be understood? For the first time in my life I'm happy. Why now, must you torment me?"

She walked closer to him, placing her hand on his forehead. Gary felt she was someone special. But he also knew he was mad to recognize that kind of nature about her. With her other hand she lifted his arm to reveal the lesion Gary denied, and forced him to gaze upon it. A sadness rushed through him. The truth was undeniable. He feared his death was at hand.

"Do not be sad, friend." She spoke slowly. "Your's is not a special case."

"It's just a scruff."

"That won't heal, and will never heal, especially if you won't recognize it for what it is."

"But if I do that, I will be different."

She laughed, "You are different, anyway."

"No, I mean, they won't want to have anything to do with me, except to fulfill their moral obligation to the sick."

"Would a true friend really treat you different because of something like this?"

Gary sat down in a chair signaling his unconscious acceptance of Yrba as a guest. He answered, "Not a true friend, perhaps. But most friends stay around only for a good time."

She smiled, then her face turned sad. She looked almost ashamed.

Gary asked, "What's wrong?"

"I feel somehow to blame," she answered.

"For what?"

"For your suffering."

"But how?"

"Because…" she paused. "Because, you only sense me as a woman. In fact, Gary, I am something quite hideous to you. I am a virus, the virus your doctor's believe to be the cause of A.I.D.S.."

"No!" Gary figured the woman was clearly insane. "A virus is a one-celled creature without consciousness. You are a flesh and blood woman that must have some need to feel responsible for other people's tragedy."

Yrba found his rationalization so true to his character, she could not help but love him all the more for his consistency. She knelt before him, clasping his hands tightly, and pleaded, "No, you listen. I come from a planet where viruses are conscious, in fact, we are conscious here, it's just that normally humans aren't able to communicate with us. On my world we live together in this creature we call It. It sustains us, and we have a sort of religion about It's power. The way we live is to take It, and make it one with us, and then, we all become one of It."

She stood up and looked around the room, like someone might be eavesdropping on her heresy. Then, she continued, "There is much more light on my world. We do not use words to speak, but the energy there is higher, the transfer of thought, crystal clear."

She turned to look at him. Gary was mesmerized by her speech.

"One day, I was singled out. No one was ever singled out before. It goes against the grain of our existence. But It spoke to me. It told me I was to go somewhere to spread the word of It's love."

Gary asked, "When was this?"

"Seconds, days, years ago. Your world is so obsessed with time, but on my world we value experience over time. No one would feel sad for existing only a second, if the experience were rich in It; because in It, experience is timeless."

Gary said sarcastically, "That *sounds* nice."

"I know," returned Yrba. "Here, you don't have the direct experience of It. It is a shame, because I now understand that here Time is everything, and it is Time that makes for experience."

"Then what are you doing?"

She answered, "The truth is, I am killing you, when I meant only to love you."

Gary shook his head in an effort to wake himself back into reality. He chuckled to himself. Either he was crazy, or she was crazy, or perhaps the most likely explanation for his circumstance was that the whole fucking world had lost its mind. He stood and began to walk into the kitchen. He said, "Let me make you something to eat."

Yrba shouted, "Wait! You don't believe me, do you?"

"What does it matter?"

She said in a booming voice, "It matters that you believe."

Then, quite suddenly, the world Gary saw changed into something different, that he recognized and felt comfortable with, but was completely unfamiliar. He was surrounded by thousands of lights in motion. Living lights that were aware, but without reason as he understood it, or words to express themselves. Instead, they communicated with feeling, and the feeling they imparted to him was one of home, and welcome, and don't worry, friend…you are here with us.

Nothing changed to show time. There was a sun. It was bright and constant and filled the sky. But it did not move across the sky. It burned steady.

Gary felt himself dissolve, and at first it panicked him. And the lights formed when needed and said to him in their silent way, "Do not be afraid." A drone like music filled the air, and Gary finally closed his eyes to reason in an effort to calm the fear in his body. He was slipping away, and to his surprise, it felt wonderful.

Then, he felt himself falling, falling back to his regular world. The pull of gravity was strong and a thin plasma of light was pulled away from the world he experienced. Two pieces broke free, and flew across the black expanse of space. They mingled together in travel, alone, but sharing purpose and emotion. They were on a mission, a mission of love, a mission of contact.

It grew cold. The light of the sun faded to a tiny point source in the distance. Still steady, but less intense. Ice formed around the center of their being. Out, in the far reaches of space, they had only the memory of living with others. It was so quiet, so lonesome.

And then their direction changed. They returned, but to a different place. They moved slowly at first, then faster as the sun grew larger and they began to heat up and shine. How long had they been frozen in space? How long had it been since their orders were given? Once again in motion, time began to matter. And they saw the blue-green jewel of the planet Earth traveling silent blow them.

A fire burned in the heart of that dark globe. Down into the blackness they fell together, the atmosphere sparking the signal of their arrival. There sat Gary, alone on his back deck, just hoping for something to happen. And from across the vast expanse of time and space he returned to himself with help it seemed to make his dream a reality. Together they smashed into his soul, and Nature began to play with herself.

Everything suddenly turned black, for Gary's mind was completely silent. He was alone. He was back in his body.

"Gary," whispered Yrba, as she shook him gently. He had passed out on the floor, and she was trying to wake him back to consciousness.

Slowly he opened his eyes again to the only world he thought he ever knew. Yrba glistened in the dim light of Earth. They had been so far together. She was his companion, and knew him inside out. And he knew her, also. He knew that she was telling the truth when she said she had come to help him.

"You drunk, or what?" she laughed as he stretched to get up. She had been a witness to his recollection, and thought it was funny the way he over dramatically reacted to the realization.

"I just had the most remarkable experience."

"Can you share it?"

Gary thought for a moment. "I could share the images, but somehow it seems the real meaning of it was in the feeling it aroused in me. I don't know; it's fading now."

Yrba gave him a supportive hug. "I'm sure it doesn't matter."

Gary asked, "What was I doing?"

Yrba replied, "I hope you were planning to make me something to eat."

"Aw, yes," he remembered. "Food." His eyes glistened with familiarity for his new found, age old, friend. "Why have you chosen to be homeless?"

"Homeless?"

"I mean, living on the street."

"I rather think of it as having many homes, being welcome many places."

"I doubt if people knew what you were they would welcome you."

"You're probably right. I didn't expect it to be like this. That's why I'm so careful how I present myself. You, in fact, are the only person in ten years able to recognize me. I was beginning to think I was crazy."

"Tell me about it. I can't tell you how much of a relief it is to know someone who sees me for something beneath my skin." Gary poached two eggs, and made some toast for his guest.

Yrba sat in the breakfast nook, looking through the large picture window out onto the deck, and beyond to a grove of exotically weather-sculptured Eucalyptus trees off in the distance. She watched Gary serve her and a melancholy filled her soul. She had come with the best intention to teach this world how to love, and instead, she caused fear, hatred, suffering, and death.

Why had It not warned her that her purpose would be so misunderstood? On her world, It was all there was, and It always remained. It was an honor to be part of It, for however long. No one thought at all about themselves. But here on Earth, where It's light is far away, individuals are what count, and she was killing off individuals. They clung to existence like it was everything. It was around them, and they were part of It, but here there was no value in being part of something not seen.

The self was all that mattered, and even though nowhere in the universe could an example be found where the incarnated self existed ahead of its abstract, individuals still maintained that their particular existence mattered more than all else. Not one example, in all of space, where the individual of a species was more important than the species in general, not in the insect world, not in the plant world, and not in the animal world, yet this belief was maintained by humans.

And humans are animals; no disgrace in that, thought Yrba. If they were not flesh and blood, she would have no effect on them. But they could be infected and die, and that reality scared them, unfortunately not into the effort of loving, but into hideous feats of self-perseverance.

She hoped Gary would be different. She did not come to destroy him out of malice, even though, all things must in their time pass away. She came only to give him pause, to make the best use of the time he still had left.

Gary brought her the breakfast he prepared. She thanked him and ate it with gusto. He watched the woman devour the food and took note that she was indeed hungry. If she was a phantom, she was awfully real to be so starved.

When she finished, Yrba thanked her host for his generosity, even if she did have to almost beg for it. Gary boiled water for some tea. The sky was overcast, and the companions sat inside the warm house sipping hot tea, and talking philosophically.

Yrba asked, "Why do you think people are afraid of dying from A.I.D.S.?"

"You mean, why are they afraid of you?"

"It's the same thing."

"But from a much different view."

"And what does that matter, any view of a mountain, is a mountain."

"Except when one view happens to be from lying face down in the dirt. Then a mountain can appear flat as a plain."

Yrba laughed, "Is that how people see me?"

"I don't know. My people have never been able to understand why there is disease. You say It doesn't know anything about suffering, that everything in the Light is good and in its place. But here, here everything seems out of place, chaotic. Our science even claims that disorder is the nature of things."

"But then why do you call it disorder?"

"I guess, because it doesn't conform to our idea of simplicity."

"But It doesn't claim to be simple."

"Well, that's a problem then. Our idea of something true, is something simple."

Yrba giggled. "I know that I am just a one-celled creature, but that seems like the philosophy of a bumpkin."

"Somehow, it did come out that way. Normally, it makes sense that truth will be basic."

"Basic, yes. But not necessarily simple. From Its point of view, of course, it's simple. It is just Itself. For that matter, you are simple too. Only when you try to understand yourself as It, does a problem arise. You are not It."

"But I hope to be."

"To become, you mean? There's not enough time for us to become any-thing. If you're lucky, you'll have just enough time to shift your awareness to see what you are. That's enlightenment."

"So you do feel someone can be saved."

"Saved? Your language is so full of mystery. From what would someone have to be saved?"

"From evil?"

"You don't know, I guess. I'm supposed to be evil—why ask me?"

"Because other people won't talk about these things until they have nothing else to live for."

"Too bad for them, to think about life only when it's over."

"At least they try."

"I want you to think about it now."

"Then why won't you answer my questions?"

"I did."

"Huh?"

"I said. I did answer your question. It all has to do with your point of view."

As Yrba finished speaking her truth, the phone rang.

"Damn," said Gary. He walked into the other room to answer the call. "Hello."

"Hello, Gary. This is Charlene."

"Hey, Charlene. Why are you calling so early?"

"Is something wrong?"

"No."

"You sound different."

"I've been talking to a friend of mine."

"Anyone I know?"

"I don't think so. Her name is Yrba." Gary looked back into the kitchen and was startled to see that Yrba was gone.

"A woman?"

"Yeah." Gary said in a soft voice to himself, "I wonder where she went?"

"Gary?"

He forced himself to concentrate on Charlene. "Yeah, Charlene, I'm here. I've just had the weirdest experience."

"You seem to be having a lot of those lately."

He laughed. "Thank you, mom. Anything else you want to say."

"I didn't mean it that way. I just meant that we've been noticing you acting a little strange lately. Is everything all right?"

"It's about the same as it ever was."

They both laughed. Their lives always did seem the same, no matter how much they tried to make a difference.

"Well," she continued, "the reason I'm calling is to find out if you are going to the Mayor's reception for the Art Festival?"

"Why I hadn't thought about it."

"It's on Friday night. Do plan to come. And see if Josh will go with you."

"Why are you so anxious for us all to go?"

"I'm covering it for the paper and I'll have a good table. It should be a lot of fun."

"Sounds like something different, anyway. I'll talk to Josh about it this evening."

"How you two getting along?"

"I've been feeling kinda funny lately, but he seems to be head over heals in love."

"Be gentle with him. You dog."

"I don't know...I, I like him a lot. I think it's got more to do with me not knowing what I want."

"That's my Gary. Never happy."

"That's enough."

"Ooo..."

"I didn't mean it that way."

"Well, if I don't talk to you before, I'll see you guys Friday."

"Sounds good."

"Bye."

"Good-bye, Charlene."

Gary walked back into the kitchen. The dishes and pans were cleaned, dried, and back in the shelf. Yrba had done that without making a noise. Or, he wondered, had she ever been there at all?

HERESY

Charlene decided to stop by Philip's apartment on her way home from work. As she rang the bell, she could see him through the window lying down on his couch watching the evening news on television. He answered the door in boxer shorts, which didn't surprise her, since Philip was notorious for wearing nothing at all.

"Hey, Charlene," he said in warm greeting. "This is a surprise."

"I hope I'm not interrupting anything," said Charlene with her characteristic politeness she so often hated in herself. "I was on my way home from work, and I wanted to ask you about going to a party with me."

"Girl; you know me and a party! How could I resist?"

"The Mayor is throwing a reception for the Chinese Arts Festival, which the paper wants me to cover. I asked Josh and Gary to come, but I was hoping you'd come as well."

"Those two?"

"Surely, Philip, if I'm not jealous, you shouldn't be."

"I don't have to be jealous not to want to be around them."

"Who don't you want to be around?"

"No one, in particular. I get along with Gary, and Josh, just fine. I just don't like it when they act so in love."

Charlene laughed. "Believe me, I can relate. But what can you do? Like they say, love is blind, and I'm certain they don't know how they look to others."

"It wouldn't be so bad, if it wasn't so obvious how it's going to turn out."

"What do you mean?" asked Charlene.

"I mean," said Philip, "I've never known two men to stay in love like that for long. Give it a few months maybe, at most. The infatuation will wear off and we'll start hearing how the other guy turned out to be different that expected. It always happens that way, and some guys never learn that it wasn't their buddy that all of a sudden changed. It's just that blinding power of lust faded long enough to see what's real."

"You think Josh and Gary won't get along."

"Hum, who knows for sure? Maybe, they will. But I tell you one thing, it's pretty rare for two guys to stay in love like that for very long. When they're in love, they always make it sound like they'll be in love forever. Unfortunately, the real world is a poor witness for their optimism."

"Oh well," sighed Charlene. "So you don't want to go?"

"No, I didn't say that. I'm not overjoyed in seeing my ex make a fool of himself, but I'd like to go all the same. You want me to bring my camera?"

"Yea, if you would."

"When is it?"

"Tomorrow night. I'll pick you up at eight."

"You in a rush to run off?" He stretched out on the couch and grabbed his thickening crotch playfully.

Charlene blushed with embarrassment. She and Philip had fooled around on several occasions, but only after being out all night and drinking. While she always had fun, the next day it always felt like the result of an accident rather than a purposeful advance on Philip's part. She felt grimy from being at work all day, and really wasn't in the mood to have sex. She walked over to Philip and slapped his hand gently.

"Now stop that!" she scolded. "Is that any way to treat a lady? You need to work on getting a little more subtlety into your seduction. That kind of behavior might work fine with a man, but a woman is a different kind of…"

He stopped her in mid-sentence. "I've seen how different you can be, so don't give me any of your highfalutin moralizing. You're just not horny enough to appreciate what I have to offer, because I've seen you when it's different."

Charlene couldn't deny that on at least one occasion she had actually tried to rape him. Of course, she claimed he'd given off signals of wanting to be sexual with her, so her aggressiveness was justified in fun. And Philip did want to be with her, though, she was only a little shy of acting like a bitch in heat.

She said, "You win. I owe you one."

"With interest," he added.

"With interest," she agreed.

That evening was Josh's night to volunteer at the Project. Jacole was disturbed, and short tempered. He had met earlier in the day with the City Council in an attempt to secure additional funding for the work he was trying to do. As usual, there was little money, and even less support, despite the reality that daily the number of people needing help increased relentlessly.

Josh's work was varied; menial, by highbrow standards, but in fact, there is nothing lower than an unclean place to live. Josh would do what was needed: clean the bathrooms, change beds, update the computer, answer the phone, and, on occasion, lend a supportive hand to someone all alone, and afraid to watch their world crumble.

The Project was located in an old Victorian style house near the Gay ghetto of town. The waiting room was once the parlor. Old couches lined the smudged walls without windows. Josh once tried to wash them clean, but the dirt was too deeply ground into the paint.

Many of the people who came for help were poor and dirty, the outcasts of society. They were drug addicts, and park bums: people who had always felt sick, but only now had the bodily proof for all to see. The grimy room made them feel at home.

Josh asked Jacole to buy some paint, but that was the least of the director's worries. People relied on the Project for a place to rest, eat, find counsel, and most of all, to get a handout of what had to pass for them as love. Painting the walls was the least of his worries, yet Josh knew that somehow freshly painted walls would make a difference. San Diego is a beautiful city. Some call it paradise. Inside the Project walls, however, it was Calcutta.

The staff was made up of different professionals from the community who would generously donate their time. Most were young, and handsome. In particular, one attorney, Gerald Carter, was a striking example of the beautiful characteristics in his relaxed clothes that fit just right, his strong physique, clear face, and perfectly combed hair. His smile alone, made everything near him pale by comparison; the whole man cast light on the flawed world around him revealing the ugly reality of its less superficial nature.

Most of the clients, however, looked forward to seeing Carter. One once told Josh, he didn't feel like he belonged there, there with all the riffraff that looked like they deserved to be sick. Seeing Carter walk into the room he thought, now there's someone I can identify with, someone healthy and strong.

Josh thought, there is someone you would like to be like again, but you are not healthy and strong, and Carter knows that. He spends one night a week here as his obligation to help those in need, those like you who will never again be part of the mainstream which is moving quickly off in a different direction while your spirit flows into a cesspool, to putrefy, and eventually dry up and be forgotten.

Carter's neat appearance was just his way of protecting himself when he came to the Project. In a ritual he would make himself look good, he thought, in order to give the people something nice to be around, but subconsciously, he made himself look good to provide a shield against his own fear of bodily deterioration. The people he helped were diseased, and he looked for disease in himself, but for now felt safe, and clean, and alive…for now.

Jacole had a very difficult job. Not only did he have to answer to a part time Board of Directors who never thought he did enough, but his scandalous past didn't help much, because even though he claimed that it was the desire of most straight people for the complete destruction of gays that made it difficult to get funding for the work that needed to be done, many on the Board felt that it was because of his sordid past that many people thought the Project was an unworthy cause.

Josh seldom saw this other side of Jacole. Occasionally, he would be in a bitchy mood, but most of the time Jacole was very sincere, and committed to helping the people he served. Each week he would work many long hours over what seemed reasonable to expect. He would get tired, and cranky, and still, he would be there helping Josh change a bed, or give out information to a first time caller over the phone. Jacole was a servant. He served to a fault, like it was his penance for past mistakes.

A counseling group was about to begin for people who weren't yet sick, but had just found out they were positive for having been exposed to the virus. These groups were always the most nervous and uncomfortable, especially when a full-blown case of A.I.D.S. entered painfully into the waiting room. The one's with severe skin lesions were the most disturbing to the newcomers, because they seemed to be marked like leapers. And the new colonists, instead of realizing that their reaction now could very well seal their own future fate, would often recoil and dissociate themselves.

In such situations, Josh would make an extra effort to go out into the room and talk to the sick man like he was still a person, with some good life to offer besides one running scared out of fear. Granted, some of the men were mentally, as well as physically ill. They were bitter, and it wasn't easy being pleasant around them. But Josh always made the effort. He felt guilty when he thought how they deserved their fate, even when it looked to be the case.

That night there was a young kid in the room. Josh thought. He was probably in his early twenties. There really should have been no reason for him to be there. The knowledge was out how to protect oneself against the virus. Why, Josh wondered, had this boy not been careful? Did he think he was invincible? Did Josh believe the same? The boy did look like him. But Josh didn't want to deal with it. He buried the feeling down with the rest of life he was hiding from. To deal with the source of his action was too complex. It was easier to blame fate for the course his life took.

Jacole put his arm on Josh's shoulder. The phone was ringing, and Josh was ignoring it as he stared out into the room at the young man.

"Nice looking, huh," said Jacole referring to the boy he thought correctly Josh was thinking about.

"It's a shame," said Josh.

"Yeah," agreed Jacole. Then, he added, "And he's so cute," as he picked up the phone to take care of more business.

Gary was deeply excited and disturbed by his encounter with Yrba. She seemed real enough. Still, he was afraid to tell anyone about her for fear they would think he was going crazy. He had one friend, however, who was active in the New Age movement and believed in ghosts, goblins, and the like. Though of course, he called them the more enlightened names of spirits, and entities from the astral plane. But it was all the same to Gary who would believe anything if he thought it was true, and nothing just because someone else told him it was so.

His friend's name was Scott. And he went over to his trailer for a visit. Scott had arranged to have another friend of his, a medium named Cassandra, come also. The three of them were to have a seance in order to get behind the spiritual reason for Gary's visitation. If nothing else, Gary figured it would be a different way to spend the evening, better than staying home and watching television.

Cassandra was a rather large woman, ugly by magazine standards, but intriguing, and rather beautiful, under her mysterious black dress and exotic jewelry hanging loosely around her neck and arms. She wore the heavy scent of a musky perfume and lit several sticks of pungent incense, she said, to rid the room of evil influences. Gary liked her instantly. She reminded him of the feelings he had as a child when his mother would read him a fairy tale that included a witch.

Being called a witch would not have insulted Cassandra. In fact, she was a member of the local coven, though she had expanded her consciousness beyond that of her peers to include contact with the astral and spiritual planes of existence through her mastery as a medium. She worked at a small New Age bookstore near where Scott lived and gave a monthly seance class where for ten dollars anyone could come and have an experience of the Occult.

Scott went one night with a friend of his on a date. They went as a lark, and were having a good time, until, while nothing that could be called magical happened, the veil was lifted for him, if only for a second. It was hard for Scott to explain what it was he experienced. It was like being in a high school physics class, with the teacher standing so self assured at the front of the room, holding a rubber ball, beginning a discussion about the nature of gravity. Everyone whose been to school has the memory of the teacher dropping that ball and saying science can make claim to explain the world because certain things always happen, like…and then the ball would drop. Gravity always worked.

But what, if to everyone's surprise, the ball flew upwards instead. That was Cassandra's power. Where it came from, even she could not say. But Scott and his friend had been witnesses to a world not quite as was to be expected, and while his friend chose to deny his own experience, even though experience is the only way for even the most rigorous scientist to collect evidence, Scott was more open to the possibility that perhaps his understanding of the world was not yet complete.

Cassandra greeted Gary with a shiver. Scott had explained that Gary felt he was being contacted by a spiritual influence that he wanted to know more about. Even though Gary had told Scott all there was to know about Yrba, Scott had withheld most of this information from Cassandra in a "scientific" test of her accuracy. Cassandra placed her hands on Gary's shoulders, and closed her eyes in deep meditation.

"I do feel some presence around you," she said after a moment. "It is a good energy, though. A powerful energy."

Gary asked, "Can you tell me where it comes from?"

"If the spirit so chooses to speak," she answered, "I can tell you what it says."

Gary thought, what skill is there in that. Anyone can repeat what they are told. But then he realized that maybe that was not always true.

Scott brought out a small card table from a closet. He sat it up and sat himself on one side facing Cassandra. Gary sat on the third side between them. The lights had been dimmed, and a solitary candle flickered on a small table near the wall. Cassandra asked the men to close their eyes, and Gary became acutely aware of the howling wind blowing outside through the trees. A storm was coming. He shook with cold, and anticipation.

Cassandra spoke calmly and softly a prayer to bless their attempt at contacting the spirit world. The clarity of her words began to fade as Gary's concentration turned inward. He felt a comfort, a rest he had not known in years, but seemed familiar. For a while random thoughts flowed through his mind, but then they turned from abstract ideas into the more physical emotion of color, and finally, they vanished all together. He was floating in the blackness of the void's womb. It was calm, warm, and peaceful there. No activity. No strife. Just a complete, loving feeling of belonging.

Suddenly, it grew hot and he began to sweat profusely. He opened his eyes and the room was ablaze with a burning white light. He saw Cassandra and Scott sitting peacefully, their hands touching at the center of the table. They seemed unaware of the light's presence. He tried to say something, but he could not speak. His body was paralyzed. Across the table from him floated the divine vision of Yrba, still the Black woman from the park, but illuminated. She raised her transfigured hands into the religious position of acceptance; no stigmata, no moon, no serpents, no thousand faces, no religious symbolism at all, only beauty, and a most powerful love, flowed from the palms of her hands. Tears streamed down Gary's face. The woman spoke, but it was Cassandra's voice he heard.

"Dear one," she said. "I love you."

Gary's eyes bugged wide open. He could not take in enough of her beauty. He felt himself rushing outward, and thought he would surely explode. He tried hard to shake the table, or shout: anything to have his friends open their eyes. They were missing the vision. But their eyes stayed tightly closed.

Cassandra continued in an otherworldly voice, "The Plague of Love has come to heal."

Gary understood the contradiction, but Cassandra was confused by the message.

In her normal voice she asked, "Please spirit, I don't understand. How can a plague heal?"

There was empty silence.

Speaking to Scott, she said, "It's not clear. I'm getting so much information I can't translate into words."

Scott, still with his eyes closed, agreed. Gary could scream. Yrba then spoke again through Cassandra.

"Love," said Cassandra as a term of endearment, her eyes fixed on Gary with recognition, and hope. "Spread the word."

The spirit smiled, and like a little child, raised her one hand and blew Gary a tender kiss.

"I don't get it," said Cassandra in her own frustrated voice. She opened her eyes, and saw Gary in what looked like a hypnotic trance. He was silently mouthing Yrba's last words.

Alarmed, Cassandra said, "Scott, I think something's wrong with your friend."

Together they frantically prayed and healed, and managed to bring Gary back into reality, but when he told them what he had experienced, they both looked at him with more than a little skepticism. Cassandra believed she was the most spiritually evolved. If a vision was to be had, surely she would have been the most likely to receive it. Scott agreed that maybe the whole thing had been a bad idea. But Gary was supremely blissful. He could barely hear the chatter of his friends. Yrba was real. Now, there could be no doubt for him.

The Mayor's reception for the Chinese Arts Festival was most likely the first time in the city's history that almost every special interest group was asked to attend a function, and all of them accepted. Of course, the idea of the Arts Festival had been criticized by some as a waste of money better spent on repairing the deteriorating sewer system, or helping the homeless, but now that the events were to begin everyone put aside their reservations and joined in for the party. What else could they do?

Charlene picked up Philip who looked stunning in his black tie attire. She wore an equally flattering black dress with a Chinese design tastefully sequined on each shoulder. Driving to the new Convention Center where the party was to be held, Charlene asked Philip if he thought Gary had been acting a little strange lately.

She said, "Ever since we got back from San Felipe, he just hasn't been himself."

"Isn't that where he and Josh got together? That could be it."

She shook her head, "I don't think it's Josh. Even he's mentioned to me about how weird Gary acts sometimes. I don't remember him ever being so distant."

"Well, I've seen him kinda get into himself before."

"I hope that's all it is."

"Have Josh and him been getting along? You know, for men, the first few months are the hardest."

"I think Josh is really in love. Being honest, sometimes it makes me a little jealous. From what I hear, it's Gary that's not so anxious for more commitment."

"Gary's a free spirit. It will be some feat for Josh to pin him down."

They parked the car, and on the way into the building Charlene saw some of her colleagues from the paper and walked over to greet them. Philip stayed off to the side and lit up a cigarette. Taking a drag of the killer smoke he watched his date as she conversed with her friends. Charlene was a stunning woman, not beautiful in a traditional way, but striking in physical presence. It was rare that a woman could excite Philip like a man, but Charlene exuded an energy that clearly turned him on. Most men found her too assertive, but that's exactly what Philip liked about her.

Before long, she realized he wasn't with her and she called him over to meet her friends. She introduced him, and they eyed him up and down, and without a word nodded their approval to her for a choice pick. Philip was well aware of the ritual but wasn't used to it with straight people. Maybe human nature is more consistent than human prejudice will allow most people to admit.

Inside, the room had been decorated to resemble a Chinese temple. The theme was the Confucian ideal of the gentleman. And with Taoist simplicity this theme was put forth in the context of present day Communism. Only in America, could a designer so dissociate themself from ideology, so as to mix what would appear to be conflicting views on life into a cohesive interior that blended these views with harmony. The room made all who attended feel special. It was a reconciliation of all the city's diverse groups…and began as the Mayor's greatest political success.

Philip and Charlene sat at their table and sipped a glass of wine while they waited for the others to arrive. Not after too long, Gary showed up, alone, which surprised Charlene.

"Where's Josh?" she asked.

Gary seemed unconcerned. He said, "Oh, he's here somewhere. He said he had to do something with Jacole, but he'd be right over."

"Jacole?"

"You know, that queen who runs the Plague Project."

Philip complained, "Why do you always have to put him down? He's doing something most people wouldn't want to take the time to do."

"Because he's self-serving," snapped Gary. "I'll give him credit for what's due, but believe me, he's not doing anything out of love. His own glory, maybe, but not love. Of course, that's what social life's all about." He looked at Charlene.

"That, at least," she admitted, "is what people want to read about."

"Waiter!" Philip called to a caterer passing by, "A glass of wine, please." He pointed to Gary.

"Thanks," said Gary, taking the wine. He took a long look at Philip and said, "You sure look good tonight."

"Thanks," Phil responded. "I like to show my appreciation for having the chance to come."

Turning a sly eye toward Charlene, Gary returned, "I'm sure Charlene will be more than obliging to give you that chance."

Charlene blushed.

Philip took a little longer to get the point, but was relieved when he realized Gary was aware he had consummated his friendship with Charlene sexually.

But Gary knew nothing of Philip's relationship with Charlene. All he knew was that Philip had decided that a gay lifestyle was not for him, and had abruptly terminated his relationship with Gary in order to find himself a good woman. Gary was long since over any real emotional damage Philip might have done, but he still couldn't resist making a little fun of his old companion, taking advantage of his male pride, which blinded him to Gary's overt patronizing.

Taking a sip of wine, Charlene said to Gary, "You think you're so witty, don't you?"

"That wouldn't be right for me to say, now would it?"

She nodded.

Philip looked at his watch. The Mayor was to open the party at eight o'clock. There was about twenty minutes to go. He asked Charlene, "Are we supposed to get something to eat tonight? I hope so, because I didn't have time to eat after work."

She answered, "The invitation said light supper."

"You know what that means," said Gary. "Nouvelle cuisine, a piece of salami, a baby spud, and a stick of asparagus."

Philip laughed, "But it's so tasteful."

"I'm glad you said tasteful, and not tasty."

"I'm no fool," said Philip. "Give me a man sized steak and I'll be happy any day."

Gary's eyes opened wide, "Now, let's not carry your change of persuasion too far. I remember well how a big steak only made you hungry for the whole cow."

Charlene laughed into her wine, almost spraying Philip who was not really amused by Gary's humor.

"Now, Philip," said Charlene, "Gary's just having fun, aren't you, Gary?"

"I'm having a good time. More wine anyone?"

"Sure," said Charlene, "I've seen the menu, and it's not Nouvelle, and it's not steak. It's authentic Chinese food, and fortunately they had the good sense to keep the menu in Chinese with the most carefully worded translations. Better to be drunk, and not ask what you're eating."

"Oh, great!" said Philip. "I hate having someone's way of life pushed on me."

Gary turned more serious, "I know what you mean."

Charlene looked at Gary and recognized that he was not talking about eating foreign food. This was not the right place, but was the right time for her to perhaps get at what was bugging her friend. She said, "I sense something behind that."

"What?" asked Gary.

"You know, behind having someone push their life on you." She figured that Josh was probably pressuring Gary to be more serious.

"I don't want to talk about it now."

"Gary, we've all noticed that something is bugging you. Why don't you tell us?"

"It's not important."

"We're your friends. It's important to us."

He became agitated, "I said, it's not important. Besides, if I talk about it, I'm afraid it will change how you think of me."

"What?" asked Charlene, with Philip's eyes asking the same question. "What could be happening that would make us feel that different about you?"

"A lot of things. I've seen it happen all the time. Especially, when something's not expected." He paused. "You would both think I'm crazy."

Philip chuckled, "Who says we don't think that already?"

Gary smiled. "Well, that I'm different goes without saying. But what's been happening to me is really hard for me to understand."

"Come on, Gary," pleaded Charlene. "Now, you have to tell us. It wouldn't be fair to tease us like that."

"Well," he hesitated, "all right, but you must promise to try and take me seriously."

"We promise," Charlene and Philip said in chorus.

"I've had a vision."

Silence.

Gary continued, "I told you."

"What?" asked Charlene.

"That you wouldn't know how to respond."

"Well, in all fairness to us, it's not every day someone claims to have a vision."

Philip asked, "What is the vision of?"

Gary thought for a moment, and then said, "Aw, I shouldn't have said anything."

"No, really," complained Philip. "We're interested. Tell us, what was the vision?"

"It was a Black woman."

Philip and Charlene looked at each other and sighed. Philip asked, "Are you sure it was a vision, and not a real person."

"Not at first. But now I'm sure. She says her name is Yrba. She is H.I.V., and she claims to have come here in love."

Charlene cleared her throat, and said nervously, "Gary, maybe this wasn't the best time to discuss this."

"I told you you would react this way."

Irritated, she responded, "I'm not reacting. I just don't know what to say exactly, and it's so noisy here, with the Mayor about to speak and all."

Philip asked, "Have you told anyone else about this?"

"No," answered Gary.

"Even Josh?" asked Charlene.

"No, I haven't told Josh."

"Just as well," said Philip. "I think it's best you really think about it before you start talking too much about this, especially to people you hardly know."

"Yes, dad," said Gary. "Drink some more wine. It's a big deal, but I'm not crazy. I only brought it up because you both were so anxious to know. I'm sorry I'm such a push over."

"I wonder where Josh is?" asked Charlene. "I see the Mayor back there getting ready to speak."

"You know Josh," said Gary. "He's more gay than he'd like to admit. Especially, when it comes to being fashionably late."

The room by this time had become incredibly noisy, with the sound of laughter, and the clinking of glass creating a white noise drone like a

blanket. The first major party of the season seemed to be a complete success. Everyone was getting along, and even groups that would normally
be antagonistic to each other were interacting in a positive way. The
Mayor stood up to the podium. He tapped the microphone, and silence
descended slowly on the gathering.

He began, "My fellow San Diegans, this is truly an historic moment.
Tonight, San Diego, begins an Art Festival that places our fair city, once
only known for its fine weather and beaches, in the forefront of American
culture. Tonight…"

Then, abruptly, the Mayor's speech was interrupted by the piercing
sound of police whistles being blown loudly from all sides of the room.
Charlene, Philip, and Gary all put their hands over their ears because the
sound was extremely painful. The room was filled with instant confusion.
Everyone looked around to see what was happening. Some women were
crying because they were in so much pain. Everyone's attention focused on
the parade of protesters that entered the room.

Leading the parade marched Jacole Smith-Rodriques, proud as a pea-
cock, carrying a sign that read, "SAN DIEGO'S ELITE—YOU HAVE
THE POWER TO STOP A.I.D.S.." Behind him marched Josh with about
seven other volunteers for the Project. Between shrieking choruses of the
whistles they chanted, "SAN DIEGO'S ELITE! STOP A.I.D.S. NOW!"

Gary whispered to Charlene, "How embarrassing."

But Charlene was more sympathetic to the cause. She said, "Oh, I
think it's exciting. The world's so complacent nowadays. It's fun seeing
people stirring things up."

And for the first minute, or so, it did seem like the protest was making
a statement. But the point was made very quickly, and the protest did not
stop when it should have. The whistle blowing was particularly offensive,
because the pitch was so high and the volume so loud it was physically
hurting people in the room. All around the room people began to talk, not
in support of the cause being demonstrated, but against the power tactics
the group was using to make their point. Even people who supported

A.I.D.S. research in the city became annoyed at being treated like uninterested snobs.

Finally, one man, rather heavy set in his tuxedo, and looking like he might have already had more than he needed to drink, stood up red faced and shouted, "Why don't you faggots get the fuck out of here!"

"Yeah! Get the FUCK OUT!!!" echoed a chorus of support from other tables.

The Mayor looked mortified, and motioned for an assistant to go for the police. The last thing he wanted was a riot on his hands.

Jacole stood his ground and militantly shouted back, "People are dying of this disease *YOU* created. Now, *YOU* must *PAY TO STOP IT!*"

A middle-aged woman in a glittering gown jumped to her feet and countered, "It's not our fucking fault you choose to live immorally. Now you live with the consequences, and leave us the fuck alone!"

Charlene, wide eyed, pulled out her notebook. Never had she seen the aristocracy act so hostile, and for that matter, vulgar. She made notes on what was being said and by whom. Perhaps not for a story, but to enhance her later recollection of an incident she was sure would make the news.

The whistles blew again, and the audience's bellowing of protest grew louder and more violent. The Mayor recognizing that the police weren't coming quick enough to defuse the situation by removing the protestors realized he needed to do something quickly. He stood at the microphone and began to sing, softly and without much skill at first, the national anthem. The conservative audience, hearing their theme, rose to their feet and began singing as loud as they could the patriotic song which in their minds justified the righteousness of their actions.

Jacole and his group were frightened that such a song would be used to squelch the sound of their voice, but shouldn't have been much surprised. After all, it was the same principle that allowed them to live a counterculture lifestyle, even if they had to fight for that right constantly. To allow everyone to be free brings with it the cost that not everyone may necessarily agree that what anyone in particular does is right. But instead of conceding that the protest had failed to affect the power-elite of San Diego in a sympathetic way, Jacole decided to become even more militant and blew his whistle louder still to drown out the fascist use of the anthem to the Republic.

A conservative man sitting at a table near Gary finally could take it no longer. He jumped to his feet and made a dash for the instigator of the protest. Jacole watched the large man run toward him and stood frozen like a deer blinded by headlights. Gary realized someone better do something if the situation wasn't going to turn into a brawl. Charlene watched him squirm with uncertainty about whether he should act.

She whispered in his ear, "Go."

Charlene knew Gary had a manner that could defuse even the most volatile situation.

As Gary rushed around a different way to stand between Jacole and his attacker, in his mind the room became surrealistically silent. He could still hear the whistles blowing and the audience singing loudly, but the sounds were distant. For some reason he wanted to cry. He felt like it shouldn't be this way, that pain and suffering was happening all over the world, and this kind of reaction to it, while understandable, because as people who don't suffer much we have very limited ability to help those who do, was wrong.

Jacole was right that the powerful should help those who were weak, but he was wrong to attack them as the cause of all suffering. In the abstract, their lifestyle may be the cause, but individually, most were living the best they knew how. And while part of that lifestyle might include a callous attitude toward the suffering of others, the debt of that kind of limited thinking was already paid by these people in the associations they had to maintain. Gary understood they did not hate because they thought they were morally superior, though they did use this argument to justify their action. They hated because they were afraid, afraid that in being themselves they would be destroyed.

He arrived in time to stand between Jacole and his assailant. The whistle blowing and singing stopped. Everyone watched, like people all over the world, to see a good fight. But Gary held out his arms and with amazing strength held the men apart who were ready to go at each other to the death. He shouted, "STOP IT!"

Charlene remembered it clearly, but could not explain why, those two words bellowed by her friend had sounded like the voice of God Himself, and she saw it in everyone's face their mood change instantly. It was like the veil had been lifted and suddenly everyone realized how childishly they had been acting.

Gary continued, "You should all be ashamed." To Jacole he said, "You, for carrying this too far. These people are afraid of A.I.D.S., but your actions make them justified in secretly thinking people like you would be better off dead. You are doing your brothers no service." And to the drunk elite, he scolded, "And you, you should be ashamed of yourselves, acting so proud and righteous, like you are immortal, as you sit there eating, drinking, and smoking your bodies into disease. To die sick is a horrible way to die. Your money may not be able to stop A.I.D.S., but you could at least show a little sympathy for the needs of your brothers, to possibly your needs sometime in the future."

Charlene felt her body shiver with excitement. She was so proud of her friend.

But Gary realized that all he had done was shame both sides into submission. He wanted to do more to leave them with something positive to ponder, with a gift like Yrba had given him.

He lowered his arms and said, "No one knows why life has to be so hard, but a fact of being human is that at any one time some people happen to suffer more than others, and those with less pain have the power of action to help those in need. Not out pity (because no one is that much better off—the plague could fall on you next), but out of the realization that we are one family, living on a fragile bubble in space."

It was not clear whether anyone understood Gary or not, but the situation had been defused. The protestors left, not to return to their seats, and the party became more festive after a drink or two and the prompt arrival of the food. Gary had shamed everyone into realizing they might have acted better, and they looked at him with respect and awe over his honesty, and consistency to the values he held important. Charlene was damn proud to sit near him, and Philip gave him a big hug of support when he returned to his seat.

But Gary was shaking. He felt uneasy, like he had disturbed the fabric of society, and would soon have to pay a price for such arrogance.

AN URGE TO KILL

When Josh finally made it home that night, Gary sat up alone in bed reading a book by Nietzsche. He heard the front door slowly squeak open, then slam shut, and Josh walked clumsily into the kitchen and got himself a glass of water out of the refrigerator. Josh knew Gary was probably still awake because the light in his room glowed beneath the door, but he didn't call out to his friend. He drank the water, took a piss, brushed his teeth, went into his room to get undressed and never said a word to Gary.

Gary continued to read:

121

Life no argument.—We have fixed up a world for ourselves in which we can live—assuming bodies, lines, planes, causes and effects, motion and rest, form and content: without which these articles of faith, nobody now would endure life. But that does not mean that they have been proved. Life is no argument; the conditions of life could include error.

Closing the book, he called softly, "Josh?"

"Yeah," came the mumbled answer.

"I'm sorry about how I treated you tonight...but, I think what you guys did was wrong."

Josh was silent.

"Don't you think?"

Josh opened Gary's door and stood in the doorway. He said, "I think you should support the people you love."

Gary looked perplexed.

Josh continued, "Our brother's are dying, and those people don't give a shit."

"You don't know that in every case. Money can't solve everything, least of all stopping death."

Josh moved in and sat on the edge of Gary's bed. His friend looked so good sitting up under a thin sheet draped across his naked body. Gary's skin was soft and smooth, his eyes so dark and piercing. How could this man be so distant, so interested in virtue before love, that he was unapproachable? Josh asked him, "What is it with you anyway?"

"What do you mean?"

"What do you want from me? Perfection? Because if it's perfection, I'm gonna always come up short. I can't spend my whole life like you contemplating what must be done to be perfect."

"It's not that hard."

"It takes more than I've got. You humiliated me in public. And I'm supposed to be your lover."

"No one there knew that."

"Jacole did."

"So."

"So, despite the fact you hate him, he means something to me. He's trying to make a difference to people who suffer, besides just thinking about it."

"So you think I'm doing nothing because I think about what might be the best thing to do?"

Josh sighed, "I think that, but I'm not sure." He moved to lie next to his buddy and hug his hard body.

Gary, however, was cold. He allowed Josh to touch him but without reciprocation. There was no attraction for Josh then. For Gary, his ideas were everything important about him. He had been disappointed with Josh, not because Josh had done what he thought was the right thing to do, because, after all, that is all anyone can do, but because in so choosing a path contradictory to his own, Josh revealed in action how little he knew his friend, and for a split second the veil of love was lifted long enough for Gary to realize his infatuation with Josh was over. Josh was a wonderful man, one indeed worthy of anyone's love, but not the one who could recognize Gary for who he was, not his traveling companion.

Josh recognized Gary's indifference and he said, "What's wrong?"

Gary turned and gave Josh a kiss of affection, a kiss like a parent would give a child, a kiss that was devastation to someone in love. He answered, "I'd like to be alone tonight."

Josh pulled away slowly. He was deeply hurt, but did not want to appear affected. "All right then, I'll sleep in the other room."

"It's not you, Josh, it's me. I feel far away from everything right now."

Jacole sat at his desk. He drank a Cape Cod to relax. He felt good about the protest. Surely there would be mention of it in the news, which was all he really wanted. It irritated him that Gary had been so brazen to insult the tactics. It was important that all Gay men stand together against the mistreatment of the bigoted majority. And Gary was supposed to be Josh's lover, something that irritated Jacole's zone of jealousy. Josh could do better. Gary might look good, but he was confused.

Jacole felt Gary was ashamed of his homosexuality. How proud and righteous he had stood there, restoring order. It would have been a wonderful coup for Jacole to be assaulted by one of those fat aristocratic snobs. Imagine, their true intentions being so clearly revealed that they would come right out and try to beat down Jacole with their own hands, not even waiting for the virus to kill him. The straight world felt a comfort when the virus killed fags. Each death went a little further to restore the world back to their unrealistic view of correctness.

But then Gary had to be so quick to diffuse the bomb that would have revealed everyone's true intention, so compassionate, and wise. Jacole laughed. Gary was a fool, and a greater fool was himself to allow such a pretty boy idiot to undermine his plans for the protest.

Before him lay Josh and Gary's test results for the antibody's presence. They were confidential, but it was Jacole's responsibility to tell people the result, and offer counseling in dealing with whether they returned positive, or negative. Josh had tested positive for H.I.V. infection, but Gary had not. Jacole thought this odd, since Gary had been gay since the late seventies, and Josh was only now coming out. He suspected Josh would be quite upset, and afraid of the implication such a result stamped onto his destiny.

The next morning, Gary woke up feeling much better. As he washed his face before he shaved he noticed in the mirror that the lesion on his arm had disappeared. He had not paid much attention to it for a while, and anyway, it was rather small to begin with, but even on the closest inspection, he could see no sign that anything was unusual about his skin. Perhaps, he thought, he had just been paranoid, and that the reason for the mark had nothing to do with having A.I.D.S..

He showered and made some coffee. When it was done he brought a cup into Josh, who was still sleeping but had been aware that Gary was up.

"Good morning, Mr. Stud," Gary said in a good mood.

Josh, with his eyes still closed, mumbled, "What time is it?"

"Six-thirty: and time for you to get up if you don't want to be late for work."

Josh had a day job as a shipping clerk at an electronics company in Sorrento Valley.

"Here's some coffee."

Gary then climbed back into the bed and sat next to his friend. Josh got up, and they both sipped their coffee.

The news played on the clock radio, and when the local report came on, there was mention of the activists disruption of the Mayor's reception. The report went into little detail beyond stating that the event had occurred.

Gary commented, "Well, it looks like your plan worked. You got media attention."

Josh didn't respond. He was still sleepy, more than anything else.

Gary sipped some coffee and put his arm around his partner. "I'm sorry about last night, not so much at the reception, but for when you got home. You were doing what you thought was right. I respect you for that."

Josh felt Gary was being honest. He said, "But you wouldn't have done it, right."

"No."

"Then you're patronizing me?"

"No." Gary was firm. "No, I'm not. It's a problem without a simple answer. All anyone can do is act in the way they think is best."

"That's what we were doing."

"But I think Jacole acts out of hatred, and fear. I don't think that kind of provocation will ever be returned with the kind of love you're hoping for."

"But how can you love people that want you dead?"

"How can hating them make the world any different?"

Josh gazed at his friend as the coffee's effect rushed onto him. "You are an idealist."

"No," Gary smiled. "There you're wrong. I am the ultimate realist. It's people that try to change the world that are idealistic."

"Oh, before I forget," Josh changed the subject, Gary thought a little too quickly for the full impact of his last statement to have made an impression, "tonight Jacole is supposed to tell us the result of our antibody tests. Do you think you can be civil around him?"

"I can be civil around anyone, but I told Charlene and Philip that I'd make dinner for them tonight for taking us to the banquet."

"Can't you do that another night?"

"I could, but I'd just as soon not change it. I can talk with Jacole tomorrow."

"Well, maybe he'll just tell me your result."

"He's not supposed to do that."

"I know, but it's different since I work there."

Josh spent the day at work with an uneasy feeling. He was in love with Gary. That could not be denied. But no matter how much he thought about the ways Gary had shown he loved him back, in less dramatic times, when no mention of love was ever needed, just a glance of recognition, or a casual touch to be close; these times, Josh knew that Gary cared for him. But as soon as they were separated it seemed Gary was too independent. He did not need Josh to be complete. If Josh should disappear one day, Gary would get over it being no less worse the wear for having known him. Surely, Gary would speak kindly of him, but he would not die from loneliness.

Gary was already lonesome. He lived in a world that no one could share, least of all Josh. Josh was working to make something of himself. Gary thought he could do nothing but become that something he grew toward, like a butterfly emerging from a cocoon. No effort was needed to accomplish Nature's plan, only the skill of recognizing how to relax with the world, to let it spin you into the proper place, to be wowed by the spectacle in that way gravity provided.

One day, Gary had taken Josh to the desert. He stood him at the bottom of a dry wash, the solid rock walls carved away by the cutting force of rushing water into a cavernous canyon with only a small circle of blue sky lighting the space from above. Inside, the ground was smooth and sandy. Gary had said the place was a power spot, where magic came into the plane of the living. Josh had not understood, but had come to love

Gary more that day. He had an energy that reminded him of the past, that made him feel like he'd finally come home.

At work, the mundane world of commerce paled to Gary's world of power. But power couldn't provide food to eat, or could it? Gary seemed to do all right. He would work hard when necessary, but when he had enough he would also quit working and enjoy his life. Josh could not leave his job, and so he worked until he was bored, and made it through the day by dreaming of a different life on the weekends. That's what made it hard to come home to Gary who never stopped his search for the truth. Josh would be tired, and even though Gary would never say he was weak, Josh felt his friend's example was about all the criticism he could take.

He wanted to be worthy. And yet Gary never expected anything from him. Gary was always loving, always supportive, but always completely true to his conviction about the way he should be in the world. Not that he couldn't change. Oh, how he would change, and drive Josh crazy. How he would claim to see something he had missed and say that now every-thing was different, never apologizing for the past, but also never longing for the stability that a firmness to one view of the world provides. Gary's values were like the banks of a river, but Josh's vision was focused on only the then edge of that stream that is constantly changing.

Josh could not understand how he could be so in love with a man, and hate him so much at the same time. But the truth was, he saw and loved in Gary something that as a child he had hoped to become: an individual. Not a freak, not someone anyone else would recognize for being different, but someone who knew who they were, and acted accordingly; someone who could feel comfortable in loving everything in sight because he had no need to possess it; someone that was free to move, laugh, cry, and to share in the experience of life in a way that, if only for a second, placed him in the reality of heaven, that timeless realm which is immortal.

Gary walked in heaven. He did not fear death. And because of this, Josh at times was terrified of his friend.

Tears flowed as he tried to pack a box. Fortunately, no one was around to witness his indiscretion. Was it sadness for being a failure, or joy because someone great touched him, healing all the suffering he felt? His feelings were so confused. Gary asked nothing of him. If only, he would ask him to do something. Josh would do anything for his friend. But all Gary would ever do was stand there, steady with invitation, not a word of encouragement, but the constant awareness that if Josh should not timely heed the call, he would be passed by.

With self-pity he mumbled to himself, "I will not be left alone. I will be his, no matter what."

After work, Josh went to the Project to put in his three hours as a volunteer. The waiting room was quiet that night, unusual, but a welcome sight. Josh was not in the mood to deal with people. Jacole was in his office reading a client file. Josh stood silently at his door.

Becoming aware of Josh's presence, Jacole put down the report and welcomed his assistant. He noticed something was wrong, and asked Josh to explain.

Josh answered, "I don't know what it is. I feel empty."

"Did you and Gary have a fight after last night?"

"I expected to, but he just said that I did the right thing, like he did the right thing, even though what he did undermined me."

Jacole didn't really understand, or care, what Josh was talking about. Gary had also humiliated him in front of the power elite of San Diego. Charlene's account of the incident in the morning paper had been unduly favorable to her cohort, he thought. Gary had been depicted as a reconciler, as a prophet for how the future might be in a community where people worked together in love toward each other's mutual benefit.

Jacole had been around for a long time. He knew well how to create power through manipulation. People are not aware enough for an appeal of love to get anything done. People act in self-interest, and a person like Gary would be devoured by politics. Jacole was better fit to lead the homosexual political cause. He had the goods on people in power, and while he would prefer to call it influence, rather than blackmail, he had the ability to get things done.

Jacole said, "That doesn't make any sense. If he loved you, he would support you."

"That's what I think too, and yet, when he's with me, I do feel like he loves me."

"It sounds to me like he's trying to manipulate you."

"I don't know. I don't know what to think anymore. I rushed into this relationship, this whole way of life, and I've never had any time to stop and realize what was happening to me. I felt the best I've ever felt in my life, and now, I feel the worse."

"That's love for you," Jacole laughed kindly. "You show me someone in love that doesn't feel that way, and I'll show you someone whose not in love."

"Gary doesn't seem to be affected. He's into his own thing about the proper way to live, or something."

Jacole made a funny face that said, what can I say but that he seems more interested in himself than you.

Josh understood. "I know what you're thinking. It does seem that way."

Getting up from his desk, Jacole walked over to Josh and gave him a big bear hug. "Trust me," he comforted. "This is your first relationship. It seems awfully hard, but others will be easier."

Josh held back from crying. He didn't think it proper to cry in front of another man. Still, he sobbed, "I'm almost thirty years old, and I feel like I'm seventeen. I can't get him out of my mind, even if sometimes I hate his guts."

Jacole laughed. "You should be glad you're not yet jaded like the rest of us. Believe me. You'll live through this."

Josh returned the hug. "Thanks for putting up with me."

Jacole, being more than compensated for his "understanding" by having such a hunk as Josh needing him emotionally, said, "Don't even think about it. I wish I had someone to comfort me the first time I was crushed by love. It makes me feel good to make someone else's life a little bit easier than mine has been."

Josh moved back and smiled at Jacole. "You know," he said, "Gary doesn't like you for some reason. I don't understand why?"

"I'm not surprised," said Jacole. "A lot of gay people resent me for doing something about our quality of life. They'd all just as soon stay in the closet."

"Fuck!" Josh exclaimed, wiping the moisture from his eyes, trying to pull himself together. "Enough of me feeling sorry for myself. I've got work to do."

"Before you go." Jacole stopped him from leaving the room. "I've got the results of your antibody test."

Josh's stomach became instantly hollow, and his palms began to sweat. Jacole's tone was matter of fact, so he thought maybe he had nothing to fear.

"Now, you realize that the test only indicates whether or not antibodies have been made by your body as an attempted defense against the H.I.V. virus. It does not indicate whether or not the virus will ever make you sick, or even, in a negative result, that you have not been infected. Antibodies may just have not yet been produced."

Josh stood silently.

"Do you understand this?"

"I think so," said Josh who had not really comprehended a word of Jacole's careful and studied preparation. He listened to hear only one thing, whether he was healthy, or about to die.

"Then you understand that a positive result is not a death sentence."

"Yes," said Josh, more anxious now than ever.

"All right," sighed Jacole. "Well, your result did come back positive."

Josh tried to show no emotion. He asked, "And Gary?"

"You know the results are confidential. I'm supposed to tell that to him in person."

"I thought, maybe since I worked here."

"Well, you have a point there. Confidentiality is more to protect people from discrimination by employers and insurance companies."

Jacole shuffled the papers on his desk to find Gary's results. He looked at the page, with the words "RETURNED NEGATIVE" boldly printed on it. He despised how one word could split the gay community. A house divided, he thought…And a malice crept into his heart over how Gary had insulted his efforts to help the sick. Maybe if he wasn't so cocky about being unaffected, he would think differently about the Project.

Jacole, with an honest face only a sociopath could feign, added, "I guess that wouldn't hurt anything." He paused, and then lied, "Gary…well, he also tested positive."

There was no outward sign revealing how Josh took the news of these results. Jacole asked if he was all right, and, Josh, sounding matter-of-fact said he had prepared himself for any outcome. And initially, hearing he was positive didn't effect him all that bad. After all, he thought, he was the same man as before he had been labeled. He wasn't sick before, why should he feel sick now?

But the reality was very different, once the seed of his infirmity was planted in his fertile mind, it was only a matter of time before that seed grew into a full-blown case of the disease. Josh went into the bathroom to relieve himself. He didn't have to go all that bad. He just wanted to be alone for a moment.

Standing before the wash basin, he gazed at his reflection in the mirror. A feeling of remorse engulfed him and he burst into tears. It was the man in the mirror crying, while another part of his soul watched with pity. If only, he thought, for once someone else could see this, could see me vulnerable, and reach out to comfort my suffering. But his soul was unemotional as he thought about these things.

You deserve to suffer, another part of his mind entered the dialogue, deserve to have this disease.

Do I? he wondered.

And the voice answered, you are proud, and the proud will be defeated. Nature thinks only of the whole, never of an individual.

Never?

Look around.

And Josh thought about the world, and how he felt himself so important in it. Always running around, busy, manipulating others with sometimes the best of intentions, but always with the subversive purpose of making himself more important, of assuring his own individual identity. And the culture supported him. Everyone else did the same thing. Everyone acted like they were immortal.

That is the dream of religion, to provide a justification for immortality. When life went well, God's blessing was obvious. But, in bad times, just the opposite was made clear. Now that Josh was infected, all he had to look forward to was the slow torture of his annihilation. He could be stoical, and act like a big man, or he could become hysterical and fight to the end. Either way, the end would come, with one path having people miss him, and the other having people relieved he was finally gone.

Josh wanted to fight. He wanted to see his enemy and defeat it, like the romantic warriors of legend. But a virus is so small, so arbitrary. With cunning it attacks each victim where the body is most vulnerable. No malice, or skill, is required in this. The body road signs the way for its own destruction. All the virus need do is push until the wall breaks and then enter with ease. The only defense against this assault is a total transformation of form, a transformation that might not extend life, but can alter the amount of time required for a good life to be lived. The body is not continuous. It is forever being renewed.

But whether it was because of fear, or stupidity, Josh was unable to step back far enough to look at himself with any other feeling than self-pity. He didn't want to change. He wanted to live forever exactly as the man already in existence. He wanted to preserve the form that had given him even the small amount of good times in his life, this despite the potential that by changing, he could come home and be truly happy forever.

He thought it was better to hold onto what he had for certain, than to gamble on any greater return. He was a true conservative to the end. And the end seemed a whole lot closer all of a sudden. How could being himself, something he had never done easily, and only recently began to enjoy, result in this outcome? Was he being punished? he wondered.

Then, he got mad. He realized that if Gary was positive, and Gary was the only man he had ever had a relationship with, then Gary must have made him sick. It was easier to blame someone else rather than accept responsibility for his own actions, even those he now so conveniently chose to deny ever occurred.

MORAL SUPPORT

Gary stood in the kitchen cutting vegetables for his dinner with Charlene and Philip and thought, I am truly blessed. A Santa Ana wind blew down through the city, and Gary had all the windows in the house wide open. The dry breeze invigorated him. Chop, chop, chop—the work was effortless, especially when the outcome was a gift to be given to good friends.

He felt satisfied, secure. Confronting Jacole had put into action many of the feelings he had about how he should relate to the world. It bothered him a little that such action had offended Josh, but deep down he knew his love for Josh transcended the need to protect his buddy, and Josh would eventually get over any bruise to his ego when he realized, in time, that Gary's love was steadfast as a rock.

To love another, one must first love oneself. It sounds like a paradox, until put into practice, and the more regular sort of possessive love pales in comparison to the beauty of a love given unconditionally.

Gary smiled as he worked. He was ashamed of his pride, but still glad that he would be able to show Josh, and everyone else he had the chance to know, the kind of love for which the world yearned: all anyone need do was accept it to share.

"But is that possible?" whispered the soft voice of Yrba over his shoulder.

Gary turned to see the vision of his transformation standing solemnly behind him. Her eyes were darker and deeper than he remembered. Her form seemed to dissolve into their depth, and suddenly Gary began to feel empty and alone. So much of his confidence came from the apparition of truth the woman revealed. He wondered what was different about her.

Yrba smiled broadly, revealing a set of brilliant white teeth. She said, "You begin to know me."

He asked, "Then, why do I feel a loss?"

"For you," she consoled, "to know, is to possess. But the world, my friend, is ever-changing. And it changes for you."

"I don't understand."

"It's okay."

She began to cry, which surprised Gary. Yrba seemed aloof of the world, so much more knowledgeable of what was important.

She explained, "The more you know me, the less I need be seen."

"But you are my confidence."

"Then, I am your crutch. You, must be your own confidence."

Gary turned away from her. He cried, and complained, "Why is it every time I love something, it's snatched away, and I'm left alone. I'm so tired of being alone."

Yrba touched him, for the first time physically. A powerful surge of energy rushed through his body and he felt like he was being yanked quickly into space by the nape of his neck. Faster and faster he rose until he could stand it no longer. He felt like he would burst from the pressure he felt against his heart. It was a rush of love, clearly, but he could stand it no more.

Gary shouted, "Stop it!"

And Yrba vanished.

He stood trembling, staring mistily eyed down at the carrots he was cutting. Images rushed through his mind, images of his past life. It occurred to him he might be dying. Little snippets of time saved forever in his memory, events that when they had happened seemed like nothing, and yet, now in sequence revealed a power of their effect that remained with him always. He recognized the feeling each image brought and then released it from burdening him. He did not need to hold onto the past any longer. He wanted to live only in the present.

Gary felt numb, floating aimlessly, without ground. He looked around at his house. It appeared to represent him perfectly. He had made it a very comfortable home. Then, superimposed over this world of order he saw a world falling apart. Around him were ruins and he stepped back horrified at the impermanence of things. He looked down at his naked body, riddled with sores, that ached from nights poorly slept, and suddenly he realized how completely he was fooling himself.

Gary had constructed his world so carefully, so rationally, and sound. Never would he have believed that his creation could be so flawed. He lived better than anyone he knew, and felt lonely because he wanted others to share in his happiness. Now, he realized that his pleasure was poor compared to what was possible.

Through the squalor he saw an estate that glowed with tranquility, not the peace of boredom the religious foresee, but the peace that comes with belonging somewhere, with finding a place finally to rest. He began to walk toward that home when he saw a man stand at the edge of the field looking anxiously for something, or someone. Once the man saw Gary, he started to shout and jump with joy, and Gary's vision vanished, returning him to his kitchen, though not without first making him a different person. Somewhere he knew he was welcome.

The room was quiet. He began again to chop the carrot. The noise the knife made against the cutting board was loud, the sound hurting his ears. He stopped working and went to his stereo to put on some music. Every radio station irritated him, and none of his CD's appealed to the mood he was experiencing. He felt restless, anxious for something, but without any idea about the direction his action should take.

Taking a big sigh, he thought. I am losing my mind.

The door bell rang. Saved, he thought. It was Charlene and Philip right on time. Gary collected himself, and let them in.

"Hey, Gar," Charlene greeted her good friend with a warm hug.

He hugged her back, accepting from her a change of mood that brought him firmly back to the present. Philip patted him on the back, then he too went to hug his old friend. Gary looked open and loveable, and Philip sometimes remembered how it had felt to lay next to this man, and missed the feeling.

Charlene stepped back and took a good look at Gary. She noticed the distance in Gary's eyes and asked, "Are you all right?"

Gary loved Charlene. She was always there with him. He answered her, "I feel better than I've ever felt, and still I feel like I could cry over nothing."

"Sounds like you're in love," she returned.

Gary thought about it. Maybe she was right.

Philip added, "You were wonderful last night. You shamed them all. Did you read Charlene's article?"

Gary obviously hadn't and Charlene handed him a copy she was carrying. The article was short, but it put heavy emphasis on how Gary, or as Charlene had put it, "a person in attendance, Gary Nolan," diffused the situation by pointing out the need to replace hate with love. Gary blushed. He never meant to draw attention to himself. He was only doing what seemed the right thing at the time.

"Hopefully," said Philip, "what you did was not only the right thing for you, but will be enough to shake some those people up. Even though a lot of people were mad, I saw a quite a few faces nodding approval while you were talking."

"The Mayor, for one," said Charlene. "In fact I saw him at City Hall today espousing the virtues of cooperation. It's like he saw political advantage in your position and quickly made it his own. Maybe not the most noble way to come to a realization, but I give the man credit, he's sharp."

Philip packed a pipe he carried full of marijuana. When he finished, he took a hit off of it and passed it to Charlene. After she finished she asked Gary to partake, and even though he was not a regular user, he figured it was a party and what the hell.

Charlene exhaled the smoke, and said, "You know, we are really lucky to have each other."

Philip who had just taken another hit coughed from taking in too much smoke. He said, "What makes you say that?"

"Oh, I don't know," said Charlene. "Take all those people at that party. They're always so interested in how they look, and if they're acting proper, or not. We just feel comfortable with each other. We know we're all different, but we accept each other for that difference, and support each other in being ourselves."

"Do we do that always?" asked Gary.

"I think so," answered Charlene.

"The reason I ask," said Gary, "is that I wonder if we're not just another clique, unique, for sure: not too many people like us, but a clique nevertheless?"

Philip commented, "Can a group of people really ever be anything more than a clique."

Gary said, "I didn't mean it as a criticism of us. It's just that I've been thinking about how progressive we sometimes feel. Remember two years ago when we were driving out to the desert to go water skiing on the river. We had such a good time. We were very special to each other then. It had nothing to do with manipulation. It had to do with the bonding of three similar people."

"Well, I do remember," said Charlene, "That was the first time I met Philip." She smiled at Philip, her partner.

"Yeah," Philip agreed, "I'd never met anyone quite like you. It seemed like we always knew each other, so much of what you thought about life and love was so similar to what I felt it scared me."

"I knew you guys would like each other," said Gary.

Philip confirmed Gary's good taste and added, "And when we hit it off physically, it was too perfect."

"Love," sighed Charlene. "I remember when we first got back it wasn't all that easy getting our emotions and thoughts in line. I was pretty much a mess."

"But isn't that the way love is?" asked Gary. "Despite the fact you two were good for each other was what happened to you really all that unique?"

"It seemed so at the time," said Philip. "But in hindsight, I think maybe you're right. I was infatuated, and while that can be a lot of fun, it's hardly a high form of love."

"But we worked through it," said Charlene. "That's what was special. I think what we have now is different, and I think very special."

Gary agreed, "I know it's different to be around you than most people in love. You don't isolate yourselves. Your spirits mingle and there's always a connection between you, but never at the exclusion of others."

"That's for when we're alone," said Philip.

"We're secure in our friendship," added Charlene. "There's really no need to flaunt it in front of people. Besides who knows how long it will last. I'd rather have our good times bring joy to other people that sorrow. Because you know how vicious people are. If they thought we thought we were better for being together as soon as we broke up the whole world would be gloating."

Gary laughed, "I think people are too interested in themselves to gloat over the misfortune of others."

"They don't do it consciously," she agreed, "but the effect is all the same."

Philip passed the pipe. He said, "Remember on that drive how we talked about starting a Country-Western Evangelical TV show to raise money to build a resort that catered to our view of the good life."

"Yeah," said Charlene. "We were going to travel the world looking for the best looking people to work for us. A total physical thing, forget religion."

"That's what people want," said Gary, "they want to feel good now. No one wants to wait for Heaven any more."

"Then, it's perfect for the show. Christ himself said that Heaven was now! We have to make it in this world." Philip spoke with his best preaching voice.

"Thank you, brother Philip," joined in Gary, getting more into character. "Your words are always an inspiration. And now, I think we should listen to a beautiful song by our own lovely Charlene Dice."

Charlene stood up and took a bow, and said, "Brothers and Sisters, you know how it is when you're trying so hard to make the world have meaning. I know how it is. You think that nothing could bring you joy from the drudgery of daily life. Then, you turn on the tube and see your handsome brothers, Gary, and Philip, preaching how only a few dollars can bring you heaven on earth. And it's not so much to send that money, not so much to invest in eternal happiness. Someday you too can come to the Heavenly Ranch near you and partake in the pleasure your dollars will bring, so much so that you'll never want to come home."

They all laughed.

Gary put on a Country radio station and they all sang along to the songs, smoking and laughing and sharing in the fantasy three minds created to bring a little joy into their lives.

Suddenly Charlene asked, "Where's Josh?"

"I don't know," answered Gary. "I think he's working late at the Project tonight. I asked him to come home early, but he's been acting funny lately."

"What is it with you two?" asked Philip. "You don't ever seem to enjoy each other."

"Sometimes we do," said Gary. "There's definitely a physical attraction, but it's like we're in two different places. I don't mean to, but I know I antagonize him. He wants to be lovers, and while I don't mind the loving part, I don't want to be married." He looked at Charlene, and sighed, "Straight men. I guess it's hard for them to get over their upbringing."

"Tell me!" she agreed. "That's why I nabbed one of your's from over the fence." She smiled at Philip.

Philip intervened on Josh's behalf, "I don't think it's because he was straight before that's the problem. From what I can see, he may have had sex with women but he really isn't all that straight. He's in love with you, Gary, and he's confused. You and I got along all right because we understood the need to give each other some space. When sex didn't work out between us, it was possible for us to change our relationship to adjust. But most people fall in love out of need. Well, I think all people fall in love out of need, but most people allow self-pity to define their relationships. Only a few understand the difference between being fulfilled by another, and sharing with another to be fulfilled."

Gary said, "I think Josh is the first type. So I feel trapped a lot, and want to push him away, and then when I see him vulnerable I want to reach out and shelter him."

"That's not good, Gary," said Charlene. "It's a game. You should stop it."

"To be alone," Gary said soberly. "That's something I've always feared, but lately something has been changing in me. I'm not so afraid anymore."

"I've noticed you changed," said Charlene. "What's happened?"

Gary answered, "Maybe, I'm just getting older."

Philip chided, "That must be it. At thirty-one you're really getting up there in years."

"Not that many years maybe, but my perspective has changed. I've mellowed out."

Charlene shook her head in disagreement. She said, "You seem like you can get just as excited as ever. Like at the banquet."

"Yeah, I can get just as excited, but let's just say things don't affect me as much."

"Is that all that's changed?" asked Philip. He could tell by the way Gary was answering the questions that there was more he wasn't saying.

"What do you mean?"

"There's something else, isn't there?"

"Well…"

"Well, what?" encouraged Charlene.

Gary stumbled for words, "I, I'm afraid…"

"Certainly you're not afraid of us," said Charlene.

"I'm afraid if I tell you you'll think I'm crazy."

Philip raised an eyebrow, "Who says we don't already? Is this about Yrba?"

Gary smirked. He explained, "In the past few months a force has come to me."

"A force?" questioned Charlene.

"At least I think it's a force. It said it was a virus, but I hardly think a virus could be so beautiful and share so much love."

Philip and Charlene passed a glance. They thought it more unlikely that a virus could talk.

Philip pursued a line of questioning. "You said it. What do you think it is?"

"It, is pure energy I'm sure. But I see it as a woman. Most recently as a Black woman: beautiful skin, beautiful clothes. She just appears, out of nowhere. And she speaks very little, while at the same time I feel I learn so much from her."

Charlene, in a motherly tone of voice, said, "Gary, are you sure it's not someone trying to play a joke on you?"

"I guess anything could be that. I first saw her in the park, on a day we were going to have lunch. Since then, I've seen her at the Gallery, and here at the house. She's never asked for anything, so I can't imagine what the joke would be."

Philip, who was more than familiar with Gary's warped sense of humor and skill at setting up the unsuspecting, started to soften his skepticism a bit. Gary seemed dead serious. He touched his friend. Gary's eyes were glassy. Philip asked, "What is it, buddy?"

"I'm scared. And I'm happy. And I wish somebody could know what I'm feeling."

The three sat in silence for a moment.

Charlene, ever compassionate, not at all concerned with anything but the feelings of the people she knew, decided to ask what the woman had done to him.

"Her name," Gary answered, "like I said is Yrba." With a glow, he added, "She is love."

"And yet you called her a virus," said Philip.

"She claims to be the A.I.D.S. virus."

Philip moved back, "An odd thing to claim, especially if you feel she's love."

"I know," agreed Gary. "But where she comes from she doesn't kill, she liberates. Our fear confuses her."

"Does she know what she's doing to us?" asked Charlene.

"I think so."

"But still she doesn't care," snapped Philip.

Gary, growing impatient with his friends inability to understand, yelled, "Can't you see she has no choice! The woman I see is for our benefit. As a virus, she has no choice."

"Who made her then?"

"It made her, like It made us all."

"It?" asked Charlene. "Gary, are you sure you're feeling all right?"

"I don't know," he answered. "I was perfectly content living my life without making any changes. Sure, I was a little bored, and maybe thought I'd missed my true calling to be happy, but I had everything anyone had a right to want, and I didn't have any reason to complain. Then, Yrba made herself known to me. It's not anything she's said, it's how she's made me feel that's made all the difference. She's made me want to love myself. She's made me love myself so much I'm not jealous anymore. I don't care what anyone does, and at the same time I've never felt I've had so much love overflowing out from me."

Philip and Charlene looked at each other. Both understood what Gary was trying to express. That's why the three of them were friends.

Charlene got up and walked over to Gary, picking him up from his chair and giving him a big hug. She said, "You didn't need a virus to teach you that."

Gary pulled back just a bit from Charlene's embrace and responded, "I think that's why she's so mysterious. She makes herself known only as a catalyst. She wants me to learn for myself."

Philip joined in the embrace. He said, "You guys know how rare it is for people to understand this kind of love. We don't put any restraints on each other, and still we love and care about each other more than anyone that conditions their love with rules and duties."

"The way I see it," said Gary, "there is duty to someone you love, but that's a duty that makes itself know in the situation, not something you can apply regardless of what's actually going on. Even people with rules react this way. I want to act."

Charlene asked, "What does Josh think about all this?"

Gary said, "He doesn't understand. He thinks it means I don't care for him."

"That's his own insecurity," said Philip.

"Still, that's how he feels. I can understand. If only he would be patient, he'd realize how steadfast my love can be."

"Like a rock," said Charlene. "Not always kind, but always your best."

"Am I a fool?" asked Gary.

"No," said Philip. Then, lovingly, he added, "Believe me, I wish I'd been a little more patient with you."

"I made mistakes, too."

"Maybe, but I should have worked with you instead of against you. Your way is more noble."

"You flatter me—this is getting too deep."

"No one ever says these things," said Charlene. "Deep, or not, this is the kind of love we should be striving for. Instead, by not thinking about it, we just waste time manipulating each other."

Philip agreed, "It's a shame! We waste time like we're immortal."

"That's Yrba's point exactly!" Gary became energized. His eyes opened wide, and to Charlene and Philip it seemed like electricity flowed from his skin, sending chills down their spines. "God's sent her to teach us to love like mortals. Sounds like it should be easy, but she says we're failing badly."

"How can we not fail," said Philip. "Our ideas about love come from the Church. Because of that, they're fucked up."

"It's not the Church's fault exactly," complained Charlene. "The message is sound. How it's relayed has been screwed up."

"I don't know," said Philip. "Sometimes I wonder if even the message is sound. I don't think all that much has changed in two thousand years. What if the disciples where no different from what we can see today? Jimmy Swaggart, Jim and Tammy Baker, Oral Roberts…what if these were the kinds of people that wrote the gospels?"

"Oh my God!" Gary started rolling on the floor with laughter. "Can you image? The last supper with those people all around the table. Tammy fixing her makeup. It's a miracle that Christ didn't kill himself before they nailed him to the cross. Talk about failing in your mission."

"None of them stood by him," said Charlene.

"But he loved them anyway," said Philip. "And not out of pity, but because he knew they were doing the best they could. That's the real agony of Gethsemane—that he had to do what was right for people that couldn't understand."

Gary pulled himself together and tried to be as serious as his friends. With a crazy look in his eye, he boldly stated, "And the Lord still lives in those that understand." His sly smile suggested a personal experience.

The others looked at their friend, not knowing how to take him, as someone born again, or a heretic.

Gary recognized their dilemma. He consoled, "I can't answer your doubt. If you can see, bear witness to the truth in me."

Just then, the front door opened and Josh walked into the room. He sniffed the air, making it clear he knew they were smoking dope. Josh didn't mind that they were high, but it caused him to withdraw since he knew his emotions wouldn't mesh well with people partying. Gary, Charlene, and Philip grew quiet. Josh wondered if they had been talking about him. He was hoping to talk with Gary about the information Jacole had given him. The frustration he felt with the situation translated easily, and quickly, into anger.

"You all having a good time?" he asked sarcastically.

Gary said, "You're just in time to eat."

"I'm not hungry," said Josh curtly. He turned toward the mantle and remained awkwardly silent.

Gary walked over to him and asked, "What's wrong?"

"Nothing."

Gary went to touch his friend, but before he could make contact Josh pulled away. Charlene and Philip became painfully aware that their being in the room was causing tension. Charlene asked Philip to help her in the kitchen to serve dinner. Philip agreed it was about time they got the show on the road and ate. They left the room, leaving Josh and Gary alone.

Gary pushed, "Come on. I can tell something's bugging you."

"I don't want to talk about it when you're stoned."

"I'm not that stoned."

"I don't want to talk about it, okay."

"Okay, but I think if something bothering you, you should try to get it out."

Josh pouted, which was not normally his way. He remained standing facing the opposite direction from Gary. He definitely was feeling sorry for himself, and what he saw as Gary's patronizing began to irritate his withdrawn and oversensitive mood. Josh did not understand how much hatred he felt for Gary since he found out he had tested positive for A.I.D.S. infection. Rationally, he knew it wasn't Gary's fault, but, really, he felt it was. Gary was the first man with whom he had an open sexual relationship, and now he felt destine to die because of choosing to express that a despised lifestyle.

Gary caressed his friend. He said, "Josh, something's happened, please share it."

Josh turned to face Gary. His face was red, and his eyes were full of tears. "Jacole just told me our test results."

By the look on Josh's face, Gary knew that at least one of them had tested positive. He wasn't concerned for himself. Since the plague began Gary had acted as if he was positive, both out of safety reasons and out of respect for his brothers and sisters infected. Gary had no desire to alienate himself from the disease. He knew of ancient times and the leapers, and how Christ had treated the scourged. He wanted to imitate Christ in this action, and found not sacrifice in loving the unloved, but a sublime calm that came from not fearing nature's wrath, or what is usually called fate.

But Josh was different. He knew Josh would be devastated by the news of infection. Josh lived in the dream world that is normal for the human species. What is not known, does not exist. What is hidden, cannot cause pain. Until, that is, it does. And then the world is hideously transformed by a force called evil, a force Gary refused to believe in, but was the only easy explanation for the bad luck those too blind to see the world as a whole experience. To Gary, nature was always kind, even in disaster, because what is important in life is timeless and has more to do with the way people behaved, than the circumstances they have to manage.

Gary spoke, "What did he say?"

"We're both infected."

"Are you all right?"

Josh tried to remain strong, but broke down half way through his answer. "What's different?" He began to cry. "Fuck! Everything's different. I was just starting to enjoy my life. Now, I feel dirty."

"You're not dirty," comforted Gary.

Josh's eyes met Gary's. Gary saw the hell of hate in his friend. Josh said, "Don't *you* console me."

"Now, Josh. Don't turn away from your friends."

"Friend! Ha! Some friend you are. When, have you ever supported me?"

Gary thought, when have I not. But said nothing.

"You live like a bum."

"And everything about how you live is an insult to what I value."

"I'm trying to make a world that will make me happy."

"And I'm not?"

"You choose to live by what other people tell you. But I still support you."

"Yeah."

"I do. Josh, listen, you may live differently, but you don't need to judge yourself by how I live."

"I don't! But I care about you, and it matters to me what you think."

"But you don't know what I think. You can't."

"Because I'm not good enough? I was good enough to fuck, good enough for you to make sick."

"That's not fair." Gary was deeply hurt by Josh's suggestion that he was the cause of his disease.

"We both knew we were at risk. That's why we changed."

"But not soon enough. I was new to this. You should have known better."

Gary became angry. "I'm not your protector. You have to protect yourself."

"I see that now, with the like of you being so self-righteous and pure, but all time spreading the evil your way of life entails."

"My way of life."

"Yes! I'm sick to death of being a fag!"

And with that, Josh stormed out of the house. Charlene and Philip came to stand near their friend. They had, of course, overheard everything. They stood silently together, only after a time slowly embracing each other.

Gary finally spoke, "He's not handling this well at all."

LIKE A VIRUS

After dinner, Charlene and Philip helped with the dishes. They were both worried that Gary might be upset by Josh's angry outburst. Then Gary explained about the test, and that he had feared Josh's bad reaction to the news of a positive result. Gary figured it would take some time, but that eventually Josh would realize that being positive was no more a death sentence than being born. A good life, for Gary, was one well lived, not necessarily one lived long.

But when Charlene and Philip left, and the house was empty, and somewhat lonely, Gary's mood became less philosophical and more nostalgic, not for his life with Josh exactly, but for a different life he had always dreamed about, but had never seemed able to make happen. He knew he was right to tell Josh not to panic over his test result. But he also could not help seeing the fear behind his friend's anger, the fear of potential life lost, of a world finally falling apart that had always seemed unstable to begin with. Now, Josh had broken the very thing he valued most, and began to realize there was no way to put it back together.

How could Gary not be sympathetic? His heart reached out to his buddy, and wrapped him up like a baby in a soft flannel blanket. But that affection was part of the problem. Gary dreamed of the support of an equal, or at least someone who could understand his values. Josh was immature, though not by worldly standards. By worldly standards, Josh was maturing at the normal rate. But by Gary's standards, standards that he had set for himself, his friend was a still a child, and someone that needed caring attention.

The crisis of dealing with death was the most important moment in the development of Josh. It was understandable that he would be fearful. And even that he would express some of that fear as anger toward someone he loved. And Josh really did love Gary. But he loved him in a way that Gary felt was a drain. Josh's love was the kind that took more than it gave.

The easiest thing in this life is to grow physically, the hardest, to grow in spirit. Josh couldn't change how he was able to love. He didn't think love was a skill, but an emotion that everyone acquired at birth, that bloomed on it's own, and needed no care.

For that matter, Gary also believed he knew all about love. But he also knew he might feel differently the next day, that there might be somebody out there that knew more than him. And he always searched for that. The pain for him was that he so seldom found it, and when he did find it, it was usually because he had evolved enough to recognize a teaching in the lesser actions of those around him. Gary was a spirit out of place, some-one longing to come home.

He also had tested positive, and yet, in his heart there was no fear. For one thing, he had always assumed his status was only temporary, and had done all that he could to make the most out of his life. Many people might think he was lazy: unambitious Gary trying to enjoy life, never working a whole day, always taking long lunches to go to the beach and read a respectable work of literature. That was not the life of an ambitious man, a momentarily defined successful American.

But now that death seemed closer, and Gary had no illusion that the A.I.D.S. virus would not eventually kill him, that laziness looked more like the most ambition. The sick always make the great turn to maximize their experience of life. Sadly, by that time they are a separated class, liv-ing in a world others fear, despite the identical nature of everyone's cir-cumstance. Now, Gary might be a leader. Except that his followers scrambled aimlessly. Like men suddenly stricken blind, no one could see the light Gary held as hope for a new way to live. He was truly alone.

What to do about Josh? The question consumed him.

After he finished sweeping the dining room floor, he decided to walk to a neighborhood bar to have a drink. A drink may not be an enlightened way to handle a problem, but a walk, a walk to nowhere would do anyone some good to ease a stress.

The night was clear, and the early winter air had turned crisp with the setting of the sun. Gary put on a light jacket and stepped out of his house out onto the empty sidewalk. Lights were on in the homes around him, but no one ventured into the night. Everyone sheltered themselves from the world out-of-doors, where the bright stars were still able to shine overhead, despite Civilization's wash of light to hide them.

The steady beat of his shoes hitting the concrete put Gary in a meditative mood. A part of him wanted to go out and find Josh and bring him back home, tuck him into bed, and hug the fear right out of him. And a part of Gary knew that would do Josh no good. Josh needed to live through this fear, to realize he had all the strength in himself to give meaning to his life. It was hard for Gary to stand back and watch his buddy suffer, even if it was for his own good. But he was self-reliant enough to do it.

Why, thought Gary, can I see?

But the night returned no answer. Gary half hoped to hear the voice of Yrba. She was enigmatic, but had consistently been there to say just the words he needed to hear most. Now she was not available, and even though Gary had just seen her that evening, the memory of her seemed far away, dreamlike, with less impact. Maybe she wasn't a spirit after all. Maybe, it was just coincidence that made her seem so enlightened.

Gary stopped.

A shiver ran through his body. It was like he didn't have the strength to make another step. He looked around and saw the shabby world he lived in. This was America, the best the world had to offer. He was standing in the middle of it and saw superimposed another world, one that could be, one without pain this time, one that was beautiful.

Another dream in my dementia, he thought, and shook his head, wiping the tears from his face.

From inside the manicured house he was standing in front of, a middle-aged woman peeked out at him from behind a blind. She probably thought he was trouble.

Gary was about to move on. He fantasized how he would receive Josh later. The man needed his love. Perhaps he had been cruel to expect Josh could handle the news of his illness with his stoical detachment. It was true Gary could not give Josh an answer for why he must suffer, but he could be supportive, and lend Josh an ear to share his fear and maybe get beyond it. Gary could demand less of others without lowering his own high standards for himself.

Yes, he thought. How does it hurt me to be kind and loving? Is it that I fear other ways that challenge me? That I could be wrong?

What a realization for proud Gary—that he might be wrong. And it was true that he did judge others out of his own need to justify himself. How did it hurt him if someone else made a mistake? He could not answer that question, except to say that he always wanted to help others, and always felt he failed. Of course, he failed.

The way he helped the most was to be himself. There was no one quite like him. It took time for people to see it, more time than Gary would sometimes allow, because he moved through life too quickly for them, assuming that he was unloved, never thinking it was the dust he stirred up that blinded his friends, and that once the dust settled it was their awe of him that kept them at a distance.

He would let Josh be himself, which is what he would be regardless, but Gary would suspend his judgement and offer support were Josh needed it, for once, not where he decided it was necessary. A subtle difference, but one that freed Gary to act as himself, instead of only reacting to what was happening to him.

Josh would come home late. Gary would have fallen asleep in his favorite chair in the living room. The light from the small reading lamp over his shoulder would make him look almost angelic, and the fact that he was sleeping would make him much more approachable. Josh would be tired, and over being angry. He would walk up to his partner and touch him lightly on the shoulder. Then, he would bend over and softly kiss Gary on the forehead, who would only then open his eyes.

"Hey, buddy," Gary would whisper half asleep.

Josh would just stand looking at him longingly, not knowing the words to say he was sorry.

Gary would reach up and pull his friend down into his arms. Awkwardly they would kiss, and Gary would give Josh a big hug.

"I'm sorry about earlier," he would apologize.

Josh would say, "No. I'm the one that's sorry. I don't know what got into me."

"You're scared. That's all."

Gary would pet his friend lightly.

"So am I. Because of that we need to love each other, not be angry."

Josh would look at his friend with eyes that wanted to love but were still afraid.

Gary would then reach up and tenderly touch him on the lips. He would say, "I love you."

Josh would start to cry, realizing that Gary's selfless love was a gift he was not worthy of, or would ever be able to repay.

Gary would recognize Josh's inability to accept his own good. And he would repeat, "I love you."

And then laugh at the seriousness of it all.

Josh would look confused.

"You're such a fool," Gary would exclaim as he dragged his friend onto the carpet wrestling him down.

Josh would playfully resist, until it was clear Gary would dominate.

Gary would say, "Let it go! I won't hurt you."

Josh would then give up resistance, let Gary love him, and begin to live his life authentically.

Gary relished the fantasy of his love for Josh. It was so pure, and wanted only the best for all concerned. How could it end any other way?

The woman at the window called out from out of the house, "Hey! Do you want something?"

Startled back fully into reality, Gary managed to mumble, "No, ma'am," and continued walking toward the bar.

Once there, he ordered a beer, and sat bull-shitting with some of the regulars he'd come to know over the years.

When Josh stormed out of the house, he sat in his car a minute before driving off. He had no idea where he was going. His plan had been to tell Gary about the test results and spend a quiet evening at home. When he entered into a party he felt out of place, and disturbed that Gary, Philip, and Charlene were having so much fun when he felt so uncomfortable. He knew he was acting childish, but, damn it, his whole world had just changed, and every experience seemed different from it had only that morning.

That morning the world was not exactly a happy place, but there was at least order in the routine of his life. Josh knew he had to be to work at a certain time, he knew when he would take lunch, and, depending on the day, where he would eat. He knew he would talk to Gary, and that they would make plans for dinner or not. He would know what he had to do when he got home. He knew he would go to the gym, or that he needed to go to the store. And no matter what he was doing, he knew what he had to do next, and in that knowledge was a great security.

But when Jacole told him he had tested positive he knew he was going to die, and no matter what he did from that moment on he was always aware that what he was doing was temporary, that someday he might not be doing it anymore. It made him nervous to realize that even when he did something as trivial as walking through a door he could not take it for granted. Someday, he might not be able to walk through the door. Someday, he might not be around.

Still, he was around now, and he felt strongly that he would survive for a while. He would try to suppress his fear and act like nothing had changed, but then he would do something like walk into a house where his friends were having fun and he'd be painfully aware that in his life no fun could be had without the fear of future suffering. It hurt to realize this, and it hurt even more to deny it. A dull ache in his abdomen never let him forget that he wouldn't be around forever.

And even if he could accept the fact that it was his future to die, he had a more difficult time accepting the fact that he had to die at the hands of a disease that was merciless in its torture of the person it chanced to infect. Once the immune system was weakened, the victim became easy prey for every hideous malady waiting silently and hidden for just the right place to grow. No, Josh, didn't mind the fact that he had to die. Everyone has to die, he thought. He minded that his death would be slow, torturous, and painful.

Jacole had warned him not to overreact. He had said clearly that to test positive was not a death sentence. Josh remembered these words, and he could remember Jacole saying them. "You are not dead yet." But he could no longer live blindly, and he felt like he thought it would feel to die.

He popped in a tape by Daniel Lanois, Gary, had given him. The music was beautiful. The beauty scared him, but he kept it on anyway, and listened.

He drove the car to the end of the point where there was a view of the Interstate below, and parked far away from anyone. No one knew of his secret place even though it was right in the middle of town. Josh sat down on the edge of the canyon and looked down at the speeding cars beneath him. Two bums sat half way down the hill huddling close to a small camp-fire that must have been more for effect than warmth. They looked like they were talking about something serious, but Josh couldn't hear.

He shivered, but it was not the cold air that affected him.

"Why?" he cried, as he banged his fist against the hard ground. "Why?! Why?! Why?!"

Josh clenched both hands close to his face and screamed, "Why the hell does this have to happen to me?"

The bums looked up at him.

Josh swung aimlessly at the air around him. He tried to hold back his anger and tears but short bursts of strained sound betrayed his discomfort. Like a child throwing a tantrum, he jumped up and down.

"All I did was be myself. It's not fair," he sobbed.

One of the bums, a black woman, walked up next to him. She stood behind his view and said, "You okay?"

Josh was startled. He knew other people where around but didn't expect anyone was so close to him. He turned to see the woman, dark, and it seemed in that light, dirty, with her hair under a knitted cap. She smelled of booze, and Josh found her revolting. He said nothing.

"Man, you hear me? You okay?"

Josh's response was short, he said, "Get outta here!"

The woman timidly reached to touch him with compassion. Josh saw her hand coming and swung to knock it away.

"I said, get out of here!" His anger toward the bum grew, and he wanted to push her down the hill. It made him feel even a little better to think about how he could destroy her and no one would care, no one would ever miss one homeless person that was a leech on society.

The woman deftly moved away. Josh would not look at her. She had the clear eyes of a saint with the sadness of a loving mother letting her child fly from the nest for the first time. She looked at him long and hard, and then turned to walk back down the hill. He looked to make sure she was going away, to make sure he could feel sorry for himself all alone.

Josh's attention then turned to his earlier encounter with Gary back at the house, and how Charlene, Philip, and Gary were having such a good time until he showed up. He honestly knew he was jealous of their connection, even though he would always deny it if asked. He had loved

Charlene, but the others shared something from their pasts that he was never able to be part of. He always felt the outsider, especially when they were all having fun together.

He never seemed able to fit into any situation. At work, he was appreciated for a job well done, but never socialized with anyone after hours. When he was with Charlene, even though he loved her a lot, he always felt something was missing. He never felt at rest in his relationships. And then when he met Gary, he was able to satisfy that need for male companionship, but only by losing the loving support of a good woman. Gary was an individual that was easy to love but impossible to tie down. That free spirit was what attracted Josh, but now it drove him crazy. He wanted Gary to be like his wife, but all Gary wanted to be was a good friend.

All of that was life and love, and everyone had the same problems to some degree. Josh knew that well. But now finding out he was infected with a terminal disease put a new urgency on finding a resolution to all of his longings. He was healthy now, but it wouldn't last long he knew. He worked at the Project and everyday saw first hand the dilapidated people coming in for help. It was hard enough to feel sorry for them when you thought you were healthy. Then, there was sort of a Christian dignity to what you were doing—visiting the sick. But when the tables turned, and it was you those saintly people were soon to be visiting it made Josh angry to think about how they would look at him as something to be pitied.

And there was nothing he could do. His fate was sealed a long time ago, when he might have made a difference, but chose to ignore the problem.

Gary had been gay longer. He should have known the danger and forced Josh to have safe sex. Gary was the first person he had ever really fucked around with. Josh knew that word "really" was loaded like a gun, but could not bring himself to accept responsibility for his own actions in the past. No one knows for sure why anything chances to fall in their life's path. To look for the cause of circumstance as an explanation is to live life like a fool. Josh was not able to rise above his ignorance.

"Damn!" he shouted, as he tightened every muscle in his body in frustration. He whined, "What am I going to do? What am I going to do?"

There was no place for him to turn, no place to run. He saw Philip, Charlene, and Gary standing over his death bed, sadness in their eyes, and maybe a little compassion too, and he felt totally the same, like he always felt, even though he knew his body looked like it had already gone to hell. Fools, he thought. Fools to be so proud, to feel so superior to him. He had done nothing wrong. He had just been himself, and their deaths weren't so far away, and wouldn't be so much different for them to feel pity for him.

Still, Charlene dramatically shed a tear behind the black veil she already wore in morning. Josh wanted to spit in her face to wake her up to her disgusting way of acting. But he was too weak to move, and let himself slip off into oblivion.

He turned and walked back to the car. Josh wanted to find Gary and be close to him. Even though Gary couldn't understand the suffering Josh felt, the fear that comes from having the ground removed from beneath your reason for life, he was still his best friend. Some friend, thought Josh, to leave me alone when I need him most. But best doesn't imply ultimate good, and Gary was all Josh had at the moment.

He drove back to the house to find it empty. Gary had left the porch light on, and a small light in the living room. On the coffee table was a note. It read, "Gone for a beer."

Josh held the note in disbelief. He thought, is my suffering cause to party?

Gary finished his second draft and grew tired of small talking with the drunks around the bar. He figured it was about time for Josh to be wandering home, hopefully a little less stressed after spending some time alone. Gary always found feeling sorry for himself to get old rather quickly. Then, he would be able to accept the support of a friend. Maybe, Josh would be the same.

Gary got off his stool and headed for the bathroom to take a piss before he headed home. Standing next to him at the urinal trough was a young blond boy that kept a subtle eye on Gary's genitals. The kid looked sexy to Gary, strong and tight, and too young to be jaded. He smiled at the boy, whose dick filled with blood at the attention. Gary shook the piss out of his penis and tucked it back into his pants. He said farewell to the boy and headed out. But the boy followed and stopped Gary to talk.

The boy was obviously drunk and as he talked to Gary he kept rubbing Gary's muscular chest and arms. While the physical attention felt good, the boy's incontinence was somewhat revolting. Gary moved to push him away, and just then Josh walked into the bar to see what look like he was embracing the kid.

Shit, thought Gary.

He said, "I gotta go," to the kid, and walked over to Josh who had obviously seen him and quickly shifted direction to head for the bar and order himself a straight shot of tequila.

Josh was visibly shaking. When Gary stood next to him, he totally ignored his "best" buddy.

"Josh," Gary whispered lovingly with humility. "The kid just followed me out of the john."

"I bet," said Josh. He paid the bartender for his drink and drank it straight down. He slammed the glass on the bar and turned to Gary, and said spitefully, "You fucking fag!"

"Josh," Gary pleaded. "It's not what it seems."

"Spare me your words. You know all the right words to make everything you do sound the most noble thing possible. But I believe in actions. And your actions speak for themselves."

Gary was frustrated that from Josh's unhealthy point of view he had indeed behaved without love. Gary said, "Why don't we go."

"Why so soon?" mocked Josh. "You want to leave your blond foo-foo so soon? Don't you at least want to get his number or something?"

Josh's jealously began to look ugly to Gary who complained, "I told you, it was completely innocent. And even if it wasn't, I should think what we've been through together would allow me a little more credit than you're giving me now."

"I give you plenty of credit," said Josh sarcastically. He called for another shot.

"You think drinking is going to help any?"

Josh looked at Gary with disgust. He answered, "I'm sick of you being so superior. If I want to get drunk, that's my own fucking business."

Hate for Gary began to fill Josh's heart like a virus multiplying out of control.

Gary knew there was nothing he could say in his own defense. Still, he tried to reason with his friend. "I understand you're upset by the news of testing positive."

"Upset? Why should I be upset? Nothing's different today than it was yesterday. You said it yourself, a thousand times, if I can still count correctly. Why is it people feel labels change them?"

He drank down the second shot and ordered a third. The bartender looked a little worried, but figured one more drink should be all right. Josh looked straight at Gary, his face flushed from the alcohol. He said, "Damn it! Because labels do change things." He shouted, "I am infected! And I will die because of it, and you have the gall to act like nothing's any different. And you're sick too." He grabbed Gary and shook him for emphasis. "Don't you understand? We are going to die because we've done something wrong!"

Gary was taken aback by the insane manner of Josh's speech. What was this energy of hate flowing through his friend he had never seen before? He tried to hold Josh, but he was pushed away. Josh felt alone, and his actions were going to make sure he had justification for that feeling.

Gary suddenly was overcome with sadness. He said, "We have done nothing wrong...yet."

Josh looked at his partner. He spirit was listening even though his body was long gone to despair.

Gary continued, "We are not being punished, though how we deal with this will determine if our souls can tell the difference."

"Fuck!" screamed Josh. "You are so fucking arrogant, I'm sick to death of it. What kind of world do you live in anyway? No one gives a shit about us. They want us dead! They like watching us suffer!"

"Stop it," said Gary.

Josh reached for his third shot. He challenged Gary with a glance and swallowed the drink in defiance. He closed his eyes to relish the burn of the poison and said, "Let's get outta here."

Gary asked, "Did you walk here?"

"No. The car's out back. I'll drive."

They left the bar. For some reason Gary looked for the blond boy who was no where to be seen and must have gone back into the bathroom for better luck. Josh hit the doorway as he swayed out onto the street.

Gary said, "Let's just walk home. We can get the car tomorrow."

"Would you please stop ordering me around like my father. I'm thirty years old. I can take care of myself."

Josh fumbled for his keys and opened the door for Gary, who got inside thinking, what am I going to do with this man? Gary knew Josh was in so much pain that almost anything he did was bound to hurt him.

"I can't fucking believe you," said Josh as he turned the key to start the car. "Picking up on some trick when I'm so upset."

"I wasn't picking him up. He followed me out of the bathroom."

"Right. You were totally innocent, as usual." Josh jerked the car into reverse, and angrily shifted it into first, spinning the wheels on the dirt parking lot before he sped down the alley toward the street.

"You wanna be a little careful," cautioned Gary, a little fearful of Josh's irrationality.

"You wanna fucking walk." Josh laughed hysterically. "Imagine, the holy man afraid."

Gary, in horror, then saw they were approaching a red light too quickly to stop.

He yelled in vain, "Josh!!…The light!!!"

NOT THE FIRST TIME

*T*he passenger side of Josh's car was hit hard, which killed Gary instantly. The crash also put Josh in the hospital. When Charlene got the news, she and Philip were making love, raptured by how lucky they were to be with someone that felt so comfortable. The news of Gary's death and Josh's injury upset them both deeply and made it all too clear how fragile we hold on to anything pleasurable in this life. They vowed never to take each other for granted.

Gary never wanted a funeral. His body was cremated and Charlene and Philip brought the ashes to the ocean and silently dumped them into the crashing surf. To the sea, thought Charlene, as the waves foamed over and swept her friend away. I've lost a friend to the sea.

It was raining that day and the beach was deserted.

Afterwards, they went back to Gary's house to organize his things and move them out. Philip went to buy some boxes, while Charlene, still wearing her black sweat shirt and jeans in private mourning, sat on Gary's bed amazed that the room looked so much like someone was still living there, but felt so much like death.

On the night stand was a postcard of a painting, Il Guercino's "The Return of the Prodigal Son." Charlene picked up the card and wondered why Gary kept it so close, though at the same time thought it fitting. Gary often spoke of the parable of unconditional love. She felt a great loss in her life with his passing. She wanted to go home and be with him forever.

"Why?" she asked out loud with anger in her voice. "Of all people—why Gary?"

And then was startled to hear a feminine whisper a reply from the doorway.

"Child," the voice consoled. "Sadly, his is not the first time."

Charlene looked up and saw a stately black woman standing in the room, a woman that looked exactly as Gary had described the virus Yrba. She seemed like she belonged there, and Charlene did not even think of asking who she was. The woman took a step toward her, and Charlene felt the breath knocked out of her from the energy of her approach. She wanted to burst into tears. The feeling of love was so strong it began to hurt.

The woman continued, "No, it is not the first time the fruit has been picked before it's ripe."

As she spoke she placed a hand on Charlene's forehead, in what seemed a simple blessing.

"Who are you?" asked Charlene.

The woman smiled.

Charlene thought, you are the woman only Gary has seen. And joy filled her heart as Yrba smiled.

Yes, She was real, very much alive, and on this earth to thresh—to separate and gather together all those who dare Love in the face of the dread storm that is a life.

END